KATIE NOVAK, EdD

LET THEM *thrive*

A Playbook for Helping Your Child Succeed in School and in Life

CAST Professional Publishing
UNTIL LEARNING HAS NO LIMITS™

Copyright © 2017 by CAST, Inc.

Library of Congress Control Number: 2017944059

Paperback ISBN 978-1-930583-16-0
Ebook ISBN 978-1-930583-17-7

Published by:
CAST Professional Publishing
an imprint of CAST, Inc.
Wakefield, Massachusetts, USA

For information about special discounts for bulk purchases, please email publishing@cast.org or telephone 781-245-2212 or visit *www.castpublishing.org*

Cover and interior design by Happenstance Type-O-Rama

Printed in the United States of America

To Torin, Aylin, Brecan, and Boden,

This life is yours. Live it your way.

And never forget that your road to success will include struggles, mistakes, and failure—that's just a part of the magic. I love you more than you know.

Love, Momma

TABLE OF CONTENTS

ACKNOWLEDGMENTS

A published book is the tip of a pyramid. It's the apex of a product constructed over time by many different people. The cover says that I wrote this book, but no great structure is built by one person's hands. Countless individuals have inspired me and pushed me to write this book and have helped me along the way.

To David Gordon, for your vision. We had the idea to write this parent book two years ago. When I drafted it the first time, I completely missed the mark (you won't see any of that version in this book!). Thank you for knowing me well enough to share that feedback over lattes at The Java Room, as you sent me on a different road that has made all the difference. All writers should have a publisher who is as committed to individual authors and their craft and who realizes that the culture of nice will never result in a great book. Maybe we should celebrate this one with some burgers and shakes at Chelo's!

To Billie Fitzpatrick, for being the best editor in the universe. Whenever I see your red comments in Track Changes, I know that there is magic coming my way. Your comments are always thoughtful and mastery-oriented, like you are inside the head of every possible reader all at once. When I'm writing, I'm now going to have an imaginary muse who reminds me, "What would Billie say about this?" Also, your feedback on the title and the cover were priceless. Hopefully this is the beginning of many partnerships.

To Lindie Johnson. "Sisters, sisters, there were never such devoted sisters…" Ah, how many times have we sung that classic *White Christmas* tune? I would say something super cheesy, but I know that you would make fun of me for it. So, instead, I'll just thank you for taking my calls multiple times a day and for being the best marketing director/illustrator/best friend/sister in the world. If I could clone you, I would. From the first draft of this version, which you said was "all over the place," to the hundreds of revisions, all the while managing my website and renovating my house, I couldn't accomplish anything without your collaboration.

To Mom and Dad. Thank goodness the universe picked you to be my parents. From a young age, I believed I could accomplish anything. You made it clear it wouldn't be easy, and I had to be willing to fight for it, but that anything I wanted was mine for the taking. I believed you then and now. So much of what you taught me has made its way into this book.

To all the teachers who have shared their practice with me. Even though I'm not in the classroom anymore, I'm so honored to be invited into yours. The more I learn about teaching and learning, and see you in action, the more committed I am to creating a system where you all have the opportunity to be as creative and innovative as we want our students to become. This book is to support your work as much as the success of students. Thank you especially to a few of my colleagues: Karen Gartland, who contributed her math expertise to this book, and Kelly Cook, who inspired the UDL Summer Language Exploration. Also, thanks to my Groton-Dunstable family; you all show me every day that when teachers are empowered and valued, they can accomplish anything. Also, you keep me real, and for that, I am forever grateful.

And to my husband Lon. Where do I start? I have always said—and will say until my last breath—you are the best decision I have ever made. People will always ask, "How is it that you work as an assistant superintendent, consult, and still have time to write and raise four kids?" My answer is always, "Lon Novak." Thank you for supporting my crazy ideas, always picking up the slack without complaining, and for doing my laundry for thirteen years and running. Some may call that "enabling," but I like to call it "best husband in the world." Literally, I don't tell you enough, but everything I am and everything I have accomplished is because of you.

DIFFERENT KIDS,
DIFFERENT SIZES

*When one door closes, another door opens; but we so often
look so long and so regretfully upon the closed door, that we do
not see the ones which open for us.*

—ALEXANDER GRAHAM BELL

On Valentine's Day, 1876, a stern-faced lawyer hurriedly approached the U.S. Patent office gripping detailed documents of an invention that would forever change human communication. Fifth in line, Alexander Graham Bell's attorney applied for the first U.S. patent for the invention of the telephone. The Bell basic patent—No. 174,465—was issued three weeks later. It changed the world. With the ability to transmit the human voice over electrical wire, Bell's Large Box Telephone was constructed of a wooden frame, about the size of a modern microwave. By the time of his death in 1922, telephones were in use all over the industrial world.[1]

Today, phones are powerful computers that enable us to place wireless calls around the world, video chat, read digital books, pay bills, listen to navigation directions, watch live

TV, take professional photos and videos, and so much more. And the Large Box Telephone is a mere artifact, an obsolete museum piece that no one would want or need to use. Why? The answer, of course, is progress. Science and innovation have given us better tools. Furthermore, our needs have changed.

With this enormous change in perspective on the understanding of communications technology, let me ask you to consider another kind of reframing. Think about how the education of young people has also undergone a dramatic evolution.

Until recently, students were educated using traditional models of education that were static and were focused on teachers providing a "one-size-fits-all" curriculum to all students. Teachers had a textbook or a curriculum, and they worked their way through that curriculum at a pace predetermined by the teacher, school, or district while students sat quietly in rows. Students were considered receptacles; knowledge was "deposited" into the brain, as if the brain was passive and receptive and teachers were the deliverers of such information. When assessments suggested that the knowledge wasn't deposited appropriately, attention often focused on the student, and his or her shortcomings. There was a sharp emphasis on "fixing" students so they could fit into this outdated mold.

We know now that if we want all students to be successful, they need a more flexible school environment; teachers must understand and appreciate student differences; and parents should be aware of their role in supporting schools and this new idea of "personalized" education. A personalized education is not one designed specifically for each student. Rather, it's an education designed from the outset to provide *all* learners with various ways to learn and have a meaningful learning experience.

Think for a moment about what your children are learning in school. It could be about the life cycle of a plant, the Civil War, how to use figurative language effectively, or how to solve equations. A textbook or curriculum program is delivered in a way that expects that students will learn the material using the same resources, at the same pace, and share what they know in the same way. Often, a whole class is expected to complete a multiple-choice test, write an essay on the same topic, or complete worksheets. When students "get it," they are considered to be good students. When they don't, they are sometimes moved into a different setting, or they fail, retreat, or rebel. This setup is an example of an educational system that is "one-size-fits-all." Students often don't have a choice about how they are going to learn or how they will express what they know, and their differences are not valued; indeed, they are judged often unfairly and inaccurately.

To personalize this process, teachers can provide additional options for students. For example, instead of asking students to read chapters in a textbook and listen to a lecture to prepare for a multiple-choice test (the traditional education trifecta!), teachers could provide a menu of options. Students could still have the choice to read silently from their book, but they could also listen to an audio version, view a video that focuses on the same content, research the concept on their own on the Internet, or sit with the teacher for a small-group presentation. Once they are done building their understanding, they could apply what they learned in an authentic way. Some students may choose the multiple-choice test, whereas others could write an essay, a blog, or a series of social media posts, and still others may choose to record a podcast, give a class presentation, or create an app or video that would allow other students to learn the material. In this scenario, all students are learning and working toward understanding the same content, but because they are given choices, they can personalize their journey. In this scenario, the student-teacher relationship evolves as education is moving from being teacher directed to student directed. When students don't have the opportunity to personalize their education, they may end up thinking that it's just not possible for them to be successful learners because they struggle with reading, or attending to the lecture or multiple-choice tests, or all of the above. This incorrect assumption might make them think that education just isn't for them. And research supports that many students feel that way.

For example, less than half of the eighth-graders in the United States are proficient readers. Over 1.3 million students drop out of high school each year—a sure sign that these young people don't think that success in school seems attainable. The outcomes are even more sobering for students with learning and attention issues. Across the United States, only 63 percent of students with disabilities graduated from high school in 2014—a rate 20 percent lower than the national average.[2] And how about the fact that only half of students surveyed in a Gallup poll note that they are hopeful or engaged in their education?[3] That's not acceptable anymore. It's time that schools fit themselves to students and move away from a practice that begins to look a little like Bell's Large Box telephone. We need an educational framework that provides us with better outcomes for all students, and to do this, we need to transition to student-directed learning, where teachers guide student decision making, provide feedback, and become coaches on their personalized learning journeys. If we can work together to drive these changes, more students will be hopeful about school and engaged in their education, and will persist until graduation, and beyond. The outmoded framing of how kids learn is getting in the way of so many students not being successful learners.

As new research is published, we learn more about the best way to engage all students and increase their academic outcomes. When numerous research studies suggest there are concrete strategies we can use to ensure our kids have better chances of success, we should try to understand *what* those strategies are, *why* they are important, and most important, *how* they can be implemented in the classroom.

That's what this book is about. *Let Them Thrive* aims to provide parents with the most effective strategies for supporting kids to set them up for success in school and in life. The purpose of this is twofold. First, it's because, as parents, we can use all the help we can get. Parenting is exhausting and sometimes thankless work, but it's also the most rewarding job in the world when we get things right. Although our kids are wildly different from one another, we are all working toward the same goal: children who grow up to be happy and successful adults. How do children grow to be happy and successful? They learn to be self-motivated, go after what they want in life, and rebound after setbacks or disappointments. Successful adults are resourceful and knowledgeable enough to find what they need to make their lives enjoyable and meaningful. How do we instill these skills in our kids now?

Successful adults are also strategic, because in our world it's not our thoughts or dreams that define us but what we accomplish. Can we, as parents, help our kids become more strategic thinkers and doers? Makers and creators? We can, when we learn about the best practices in education and try to incorporate them into our parenting repertoire. When you know what happens in the brain when kids learn, you'll be able to reflect on how to "personalize" parenting for your kids and help them to build critical skills for their future.

The second purpose of this book is to give parents like yourself the information you need to understand how to maximize your children's school experience. What steps can you take to ensure that your child and all students get the most out of a school environment to better their chance of success? And by school environment, I'm not talking about the architecture of the building, a school's flashy technology, or the size of the class—these elements don't predict how well our kids will do in their future. I'm talking about how to think about what teachers do (or don't do) in classrooms to design curriculum and instruction that matters to all students and provides them with opportunities to practice the skills they will need in their future. I am by no means blaming teachers here. I am a teacher myself and hold this profession in the highest of esteem. My problem is with how teachers are often still trapped by how schools deliver education. So many well-meaning teachers and administrators are hamstrung by the old framing of how kids learn and the restrictive school environment that comes from outdated beliefs about how students should learn.

I've never met a teacher who wasn't receptive to implementing new innovative practices to personalize the education of all students. In fact, teacher conferences are more like rock concerts than professional development seminars, because when teachers understand how flexible and accessible education can be for them and their students, they become incredibly energized. However, getting to this place of understanding involves barriers that prevent teachers from providing all students with options to personalize their journey toward rigorous standards. Knowing more about what teachers are up against will help you become an ally and partner with them so all of our kids can access authentic, meaningful learning opportunities that will help them realize their own definition of success, regardless of their variability.

Before we discuss the challenges that teachers face every day, we all have to remember one thing: teachers are our partners and they truly want the same thing we do for our kids. All parents want their kids to succeed, and teachers want that too. We all know that teachers have a mix of strengths and weaknesses, just like we do as parents, but in order to ensure that all teachers become expert teachers, schools and parents need to value them for who they are and create environments where all they can be successful. Teaching and learning are alterable variables, and best practices in education can be taught. Whether or not your child's teacher is currently providing options for students to personalize their education, you have to give them credit for their commitment to our kids' futures.

To put teaching in perspective, I want to start out by saying that every single one of them would put his or her life on the line for your child. We have all heard the stories of teachers shielding students from bullets in school shootings, teachers carrying students away from flooded buildings, and teachers donating their own paychecks to purchase kids what they need.

In 2013, I attended *NBC Education Nation* as a teacher. During the live broadcast, they showed a video that still gives me chills today when I think about it. They shared the coverage of the tornado that ravaged Plaza Towers Elementary School in Oklahoma and killed seven students. One first responder, in tears, said, "We had to pull a car off a teacher in the hallway. I don't know what that lady's name was, but she had three little kids underneath her. Good job, teach." (Those children survived, as did the teacher.)

When we are talking about improving teaching and learning, it's important that we value the work and effort that teachers commit to our kids on a daily basis. Before we dive into what may not be happening in classrooms, it's important to know that teachers are doing the best they can with what they have, and if we want them to improve, we have to advocate for systems that value them and give them the opportunities to personalize teaching and learning so they can meet the needs of all of our kids. They guard and educate our kids with their lives, and they deserve our appreciation, respect, and support.

Step back for a moment, as a parent, and consider that as adults, we are all learners just as much as our children. If there is something that we don't do well, it's because we haven't learned how to do it *yet*. As an example, I don't ski. In fact, I may argue that skiing for me would be impossible, and that I could never possibly ski with my husband, who in his heyday could ski double black diamond trails (or so he says...). When schools and teachers say they can't meet the needs of all students, they are in the same place that I am when I'm staring up at a snowy mountain. We, as a society, have to change the lens and realize that we can't do it *yet*, but with the right support and training, anything is well within our reach. This is true for our kids, our teachers, and us.

Our teachers are up against a lot. Understanding the struggle that teachers face daily in the classroom is important, so we can see the classroom through their eyes and become partners in educating our kids. The shift to student-directed, personalized learning requires significant effort and change on the part of teachers, schools, and families.

UNIVERSAL DESIGN FOR LEARNING: OPTIMIZING EDUCATION FOR ALL

To optimize access to quality education for all our kids, the lines between our homes and schools need to be erased. What is best for our kids is best for them in our homes *and* within their classroom walls. We all want our students to set meaningful goals and strive for them. We want them to feel fulfilled and be happy, and we want them to learn how to go after what they want in life. To do this, both parents and teachers need to provide them with options so they can personalize their journey to achieve great things. Never before has there been such an opportunity for collaboration between these two worlds. This opportunity is possible because of an educational framework, based on scientific research that provides us with common language.

A tremendous amount of research exists that demonstrates the old way of teaching is simply not working for all students. Lecturing, textbooks, and multiple-choice tests are not the best tools at a teacher's disposal, just like Bell's Large Box Telephone is not on display at the Apple Store. Making the kind of impact needed to give our children equal opportunities at success requires a personalized approach to teaching and learning.

To do this, we need to think differently about schools and our roles as parents in supporting teachers and teaching. Effective schools empower all learners—teachers, students, and parents—to focus on teaching and learning. John Dewey, one of the greatest thinkers in education, in his book *How We Think* in 1910,[4] said, "Teaching and learning are correlative or corresponding processes, as much so as selling and buying. One might as well say he has sold when no one has bought, as to say that he has taught when no one has learned." Using this lens, when our kids haven't learned, we as parents and teachers haven't taught. This gives all of us an incredible opportunity to learn more about best practices in education, so we are armed with the knowledge and resources to transform teaching and learning in schools and at home.

This framework, called Universal Design for Learning (UDL), provides a foundation to show schools and teachers how to meet the needs of all of our children while also teaching them important skills for the future, like self-direction, creativity, and problem solving. These strategies give all students a voice in the design and delivery of their own learning, and as they change and evolve as learners, their education will change and evolve with them, challenging them to reach further and accomplish more. In short, we don't set out to fix students. We set out to fix our schools.

Transforming our schools is critical for success, but it's not something that teachers, or administrators, or parents, can do alone. Our schools need to provide a high-quality, engaging education to all students, so they are committed to their own success. This has to be true for every student, not just those who arrive ready to learn; in other words, every child can become an expert learner. But in order to accomplish this shift in mindset, we—as educators and parents—have to reframe the way we view teaching and learning. We can't teach all students in the same way. We can have standards, but we cannot standardize people, insisting that they all learn and express themselves the same way. Schools and teachers want the best outcomes for students; they want to collaborate with parents to set up students for success in life. This book is not anti-school. In fact, it's the opposite—it is pro-school. Schools have tremendous power and education has tremendous opportunity. And there are things we can do to support schools. We can advocate for them to implement UDL, but we can also begin to incorporate the principles of UDL into our homes, when we're supporting our kids with homework, asking them to help around the house, and when they are competing in dance, music, or athletics.

In this book, I will share with you a set of tools that are based on the UDL framework. The tools and the framework are meant to help you understand more about the nuances of how your particular child or student learns. You will also learn how UDL can be used in the classroom for different types of learners. Indeed, you will see how the one consistent feature of learning is variability: all students learn differently and take different paths to success.

A lot of practices occurring in schools these days are ready for extinction, just as Bell's telephone was. We know better now. The way we were educated had its day, and now those days are over. When UDL is implemented, students have more opportunities to create their own path and experience the success they deserve. The way that students were taught in the past does not meet their needs or the world we live in, which is why UDL is so necessary.

It's time to focus on UDL so our kids can experience an engaging, meaningful education that teaches them to dream, to wonder, to create, and to never give up on themselves. The vast number of students who are disengaged in their education has become a national crisis, which is upsetting, especially because there is an answer for how to address it: UDL.

Key Takeaways

- Many students are educated using techniques that no longer meet their current needs or future needs.

- Parents and teachers have an incredible opportunity to work together to ensure that all students are motivated and committed to their education.

- Universal Design for Learning (UDL) is a framework for teaching and learning, based on decades of research, which will engage all students in meaningful, personalized learning experiences.

TURNING ON THE BRAIN
SO IT CAN LEARN

*A*s parents, we want what is best for our kids. We want
them to be happy, be well liked, and learn easily. The
reality, however, is that learning is a complex process that
requires attention and effort. All students learn differently,
and as a result, they need opportunities to personalize their
education. The only constant is that learning requires three
different areas of the brain to be activated, communicating,
and persistent when faced with challenges.

It's possible that certain kids are not engaged learners,
whether they attend school or are home-schooled. Some
kids decide that their education is too hard, boring, or use-
less. These reactions are not necessarily due to a learning or
attention issues or because there is something that needs
to be "fixed" with your child; kids respond to school in a
range of ways because their current learning environments
are rarely designed in ways that offer them the flexibility
they need to succeed. If we want students to learn, all

teachers have to design and deliver instruction so that students have opportunities to activate the networks of the brain that have to be turned on for them to succeed. To do this, teachers need the freedom and autonomy to provide students with options for how they learn and how they express what they know. This requires school administrators to understand UDL so that they can provide teachers with the professional development and empowerment they need to design an education that meets the needs of all students. Scripted curriculum, pacing guides, and standardized tests, all common practices in education today, are barriers that can be overcome when we, as parents, advocate for the changes that systems require to meet the needs of our teachers and our kids.

To help you better understand what it takes for kids to learn, think of the brain as a heating system. When your house is cold, you simply want to turn on your heating system and get on with your day. Similarly, when your kids are frustrated, give up too easy, or don't want to learn and do the schoolwork being asked of them, you'd like to just flip a switch to "turn on" a so-called learning button. But learning isn't instantaneous, just like heat doesn't warm your house to the desired temperature in a matter of seconds.

Here's a case in point: Imagine that you're in a snowy paradise. The temperatures are below freezing, but the skiing is great (or maybe you're just visiting for the spa for the day!). After a long day on the slopes or getting a hot stone massage, your family heads back to the house to warm up.

Instead, you walk into the house and you can see your breath. Immediately the whining starts from the masses:

"It's so cold. I'm going back in the car."

"Ugh. I hate this house. I told you we should've moved to Florida."

"Mooooom, Daaaaaaad, he touched me with his cold hands."

Ignoring the complaints, you make a beeline for the thermostat. For whatever reason, it's set to 40 degrees. A preteen over your shoulder mumbles, "Feels colder than that to me," and bumps you to the side to punch at the arrow, trying to warm up the room. "It still feels the same. Stupid thing is broken."

All you want at this point is a hot toddy, a nanny, and instant heat, but heat is not instant.

The same is true of learning. Learning is a process—a multidimensional experience that needs to be personalized for each of us because we are more committed to learn about things that inspire us, that interest us, and that help us reach our goals. And this takes time and effort. If it were instant, or easy, it wouldn't be as rewarding to achieve. The struggle, and what we have to overcome to achieve our goals, is what drives us.

It's all too easy to take complicated systems for granted and forget all the moving parts that are necessary to get a full system working properly. For a moment, think about the main components of a heating system. If for some reason one of the parts doesn't get activated, you're not going to be able to warm up your house. All heating systems work slightly differently (just as all children learn differently), but for this analogy we're going to compare the brain to a forced-air furnace. A forced-air furnace has three basic components, which must work together to produce heat: the thermostat, the burner, and the blower.

A thermostat activates the whole heating process. Once a thermostat's temperature is set, it communicates with the burner to tell it to turn on or off in order to bring the house to the desired temperature. The burner must recognize the command from the thermostat and begin to activate all its parts, including its pump and motor. Finally, you have the blower, which distributes the heat produced by the burner. If any of these parts can't function, it doesn't matter what temperature you set on the thermostat—your goal of being warm is a pipe dream.

Technically, we could talk about the parts of a forced-air heating system in isolation, but suffice to say that if any or all of the parts aren't working, you're going to be piling on the blankets and wishing for warmer weather.

Learning is a process that occurs in three areas of the brain, and parents, teachers, and schools can help foster that process if they understand the system and how it works. The human brain is similar to this heating system because there are three networks of the brain that have to work together to produce learning: the affective network, the recognition network, and the strategic network.

Knowing the purpose of each of the three networks is critical in understanding how our kids learn. For learning to occur, three things have to happen. First, learners have to be motivated and purposeful, which occurs in the *affective network*. If a lesson is not interesting or meaningful, or if our kids lack the ability to commit to the task, the learning process is not off to a good start. Once the affective network has kicked off the process, learners have to be able to build their understanding and knowledge in the *recognition network* by using resources that they can access and that

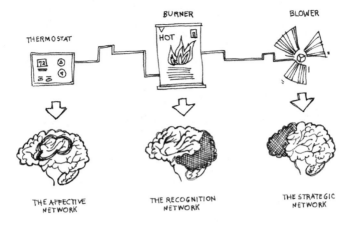

THERMOSTAT   BURNER   BLOWER

THE AFFECTIVE
NETWORK   THE RECOGNITION
NETWORK   THE STRATEGIC
NETWORK

are meaningful to them. Finally, they have opportunities to express what they have learned in an authentic way by activating their **strategic network**. To simplify this process and highlight the connections among the three networks:

- The affective network has to be motivated.

- The recognition network has to be resourceful.

- The strategic network has to be self-directed.

    ...if we want students to become expert learners.

THE AFFECTIVE NETWORK

Think of the affective network as a thermostat of the learning brain. It's the *why* of learning. If we want our kids to love learning, we have to recruit their interest and help them identify a meaningful goal (i.e., connect them to why certain information, for example, is relevant and meaningful to learn). When kids know the *why*, then they are more likely to put forth the effort. But this "getting the why" requires us to get their attention, which must then be followed up by perseverance. As we all know well, it is not enough for us to just get our kids' attention. Success, or anything that is worth achieving, requires significant effort and the ability to self-regulate or cope when things get challenging (because they will!), and these skills are a part of the affective network as well. A thermostat is no good in the house if it can't work with the heating system as a whole in order to regulate its temperature.

Learning requires that our kids regulate their emotions and stay committed even when things get hard, and that is a skill that is learned over time. As kids experience new situations at home and at school, their affective network attempts to sense purpose and value. Recent research measured the amount of time it takes to make a first impression or react to a new situation.[5] The answer? A tenth of a second. And even when researchers allowed participants to make judgments with no time limits, their impressions didn't change. So the affective network is fast out of the gate. When it's turned

on, it's looking to make meaning, set goals, apply effort, and cope with challenges. And when it's not?

If a thermostat is set to 40 degrees, the system doesn't know *why* it's important to be at a balmy 72. Similarly, when affective network is not tapped, learning doesn't occur because of boredom, disinterest, or a lack of attention, or because the learner doesn't know *why* it's important, or they don't know how to self-regulate when the journey requires more effort or coping than they have the tools for. When the affective network of the brain is not activated, it is desperate, frustrated, and unmotivated. Just as a heating system won't produce heat if the thermostat hasn't been activated, students will not experience authentic learning if their affective network hasn't been activated.

I recently attended a lecture that equated keeping the affective network activated to a cow trying to work its way through a cornfield. It's a rather bizarre analogy, but it works. For a moment, imagine a cow that has to schlep all the way around a giant cornfield to get to pasture. It's a long walk. One day, the cow realizes that it would be a lot quicker if she just plowed right through the middle of the field. The motivation is there, but it won't be an easy trip the first time. The poor thing is going to get scraped by the husks; the stalks are going to be snapping under the weight of the beast; and as it moves through the field, its path will close behind her. Eventually, the cow may panic—she's in unknown territory and she doesn't know which way to turn. Finally, after struggling and walking in circles, the cow will eventually get out.

At this point, the cow has two options: 1. Never do that again, or 2. Dust off those hind legs and try it again the next day even though it's going to be challenging. It won't be quite as hard, as there are clues about where the cow has gone before... a broken-off ear of corn, hoof prints if you look closely... but it won't be easy either. Because learning is challenging, students must continually walk into uncharted territory (i.e., the cornfield) even when they are motivated to succeed. Trying something new can be scary because it requires vulnerability and effort, and success will not happen right away.

Research tells us that success takes a long time—a really long time. In Malcolm Gladwell's best-selling book, *Outliers: The Story of Success*, he analyzes the success of individuals who have risen above their competitors to become the greatest in their fields—including the Beatles, Steve Jobs, and Bill Gates. What did he find? Gladwell popularized the "10,000-Hour Rule" to highlight what all success stories have in common. In every case, a wildly successful individual had the opportunity to practice for the equivalent of 10,000 hours.[6] No exceptions.

Even with 10,000 hours, not everyone will become an "outlier." Gladwell has faced and answered criticism that the rule is an overgeneralization. Of course, he answers, no one becomes a superstar without innate talent as well.[7] But clearly success depends on one's ability to commit to practicing again and again, to making the long journey.

The message for us as parents is that if we want success for our kids, we have to teach them to commit to something and see success as a journey, not something that happens on the first try or if they are lucky. The affective experience, therefore, is when our kids are "in the zone." When they are motivated to achieve a goal and they won't let anything stand in their way, they are experiencing learning as positive and motivating. They may experience setbacks and struggle, but they will continue to persist and cope with these disappointments, because they know *why* they are trying so hard. The destination is worth the journey. This 10,000-Hour Rule is further evidence why the affective network needs both attention and commitment to achieve its goals.

THE RECOGNITION NETWORK

If the affective network is the thermostat of the brain, the recognition network is the burner. The burner in a heating system has to make meaning from the information sent by the thermostat so it knows *what* it's supposed to do. Similarly, the recognition network manages the *what* of learning. Its job is to receive information and translate it.

The burner in a heating system has to take the information provided by the thermostat and translate that information into a meaningful message for the rest of the

system. Does it need to create heat or does it need to stop making heat? Interpreting this message correctly is critical to the heating system being able to function effectively and optimally. In other words, if the message is jumbled for any reason, the functioning of the system will be impacted—usually in a negative way.

How are learners like the burner of a heating system? Like the burner, if a learner's brain (specifically the recognition network of his or her brain) received a message that is unclear, garbled, or in an unrecognizable language, then that burner will not "turn on." In other words, the learning will not occur.

As parents, you know that if you give all your kids the same instructions, they will have very different interpretations of that message, which is a result of the wide variability in how kids recognize and interpret information. Learners are unique in how they comprehend information, so the *what* of their learning needs to be age appropriate, aligned to a specific set of standards or goals, and well organized. In addition, the deliverer of the information (typically the teacher) needs to make sure that the content is valuable or authentic—to that learner.

Some kids will recognize information more easily depending on how it's presented. Some students respond well to auditory directions, whereas others excel with visuals, demonstrations, or printed text. Some learn information quickly; others need more time. Kids may need directions or instructions repeated or clarified, or they may need vocabulary and symbols translated or explained. To activate the recognition network, all students need options for how they are going to acquire new information.

This *what* of learning is critical for our kids to build knowledge and skills, and yet so often, instructions and lessons are delivered in only one way. Often, teaching is designed for the mythical average learner, who can excel by listening to lectures and reading printed text. Although these practices are appropriate options for some kids, they don't work for all of them. In an inclusive school that values all learners, students don't have to be educated in a different setting to get what they need. All students deserve to know *why* they are learning, and they also should know *what* they are learning about while sitting in class together.

THE STRATEGIC NETWORK

The third network of the brain is the strategic network. Once the affective network is activated and our kids know *why* they are learning, and the recognition network has interpreted *what* they need to know, the strategic network creates the action plan so they can express the new knowledge or skill in a way that it's clear *how* the learning is meaningful and valuable.

In a heating system, heat is a tangible byproduct that is delivered from the blower. So too should our kids be challenged to accomplish their goals in an authentic way. Authentic products, however, require effort, self-regulation, understanding, and strategy. Also, authentic products are not always the norm in our classrooms. For example, many teachers assess students' knowledge using a "one-size-fits-all" approach such as multiple-choice tests, worksheets, or essays. These may not allow all students to communicate their knowledge or skills, and they are definitely not authentic products, or ones that learners would use in the real world. Think of these types of assessments as a closed vent. The heat may have been produced, but there is no way to let it out.

Authentic assessments have real-world application and require self-direction and problem solving. In a universally designed learning environment, an authentic assessment is designed to measure the outcomes of personalized opportunities to learn content and skills and overcome barriers.

Karen Gartland, an experienced educator and co-author of the series *Well Played: Building Mathematical Thinking Through Number Games and Puzzles*, is an expert in how to build mathematical thinking through authentic, engaging assessments. She provided an example for this book that will allow you to see how a universally designed assessment provides students with meaningful options so that they express their understanding of math concepts in a way that matters.[8]

Imagine you have a child in fifth grade who needs to learn how to calculate volume of a rectangular prism. Back when we were in school, we likely practiced this skill by completing a series of problems or worksheets, and taking a quiz or test at the completion of the unit. Instead of these more traditional methods, Gartland provides an example of a real-world task that allows students to personalize their learning journey and practice self-direction, creativity, and problem solving. In the following box, you will see an explanation of the task that could be distributed to students. Imagine your child receiving an assessment like this instead of a packet of worksheets. You will notice the opportunities for students to personalize their journey while completing an authentic and engaging task.

Task

Our school principal has learned that you are all working on the volume of a rectangular prism and he needs your help. He wants to install an aquarium outside the front office (this is really happening and will be funded by student council!). The sixth-graders are studying sea life and have asked him if it can be a saltwater tank. They have given him a list of the types of fish that they want in the tank, each of which need a certain volume of water in which to live. Now it's up to you to design an aquarium that will meet the qualifications for the type of fish that the sixth-graders want and that will fit in the front of the school office.

There is no right or wrong way to do this project. You can use your textbooks or use your devices to explore videos, or you can ask me to present to your group. You are free to use calculators and math reference sheets, and/or ask me for an exemplar if you need it.

You can work together or alone. Whatever you decide, don't be afraid to try things and make mistakes. The design, the materials, your learning journey, and the product are up to you. Once you have determined an appropriate set of measurements for your tank, you can choose how to present your results to the principal. You can make a poster, write a letter, or make a video, complete with animation.

For a super challenge, if you have a better idea for that space that would still allow you to calculate the volume of a rectangular prism, propose an idea to me in the next 10 minutes! Be as creative as you wish and know that I am here to support you.

As students walk into class, the task may be projected on the board and stacks of printed handouts may also be available on the tables. The teacher provides auditory instructions and then walks around the room to clarify directions if necessary, and kids get right to work!

In this scenario, the teacher supports students as a coach, as he or she observes student teams engaged in creative problem solving. The teacher may observe groups researching the list of the fish to determine how much water each needs, looking for a measuring tape and heading to the office to measure the area, sketching possible designs, and discussing how they will present their designs once complete. Some students are working alone, watching videos on their devices while wearing headphones. Other students are at standing desks; still other students are sitting on the ground with butcher paper designing the tank visually.

In our example, students have the option to collaborate and personalize their learning experience as they work toward a rigorous standard. The magic of the example, however, is that there is so much embedded choice. They can choose the way that makes most sense to them. They can also choose to express what they know in a way that honors their strengths, which, in turn, makes the outcome an authentic product, a fish tank that they helped to design. Being involved in a learning experience like that requires the brain to work as a complex system to commit to the task, learn the necessary information, and share it in a way that is relevant and meaningful.

CREATING EXPERT LEARNERS

As you can see in our example, an authentic assessment requires all three networks of the brain to activate and communicate with one another—all three systems have to be working in collaboration if we want our kids to be successful. When all three networks of the brain are activated in our kids, we call them **expert learners**. An expert learner is someone who is motivated to continuously improve and develop his or her skills while working toward a meaningful, relevant goal in a personalized way. Expert learners don't necessarily start with the highest level of ability or knowledge—but they never give up and work hard to reach their goals. Every single one of our kids has the potential to become an expert learner if provided with a motivating environment that values the process of learning more than the mastery of specific knowledge.

Take Richie Parker, a chassis and body component designer for Hendrick Motorsports who was born without arms. An ESPN, Emmy award–winning video highlights his journey from childhood to becoming a top engineer at the most winning organization in NASCAR. He drives a car, welds body parts, and does all his engineering work on his computer, with his feet. To be successful, he's had to learn how to do things "his way," and he has overcome a number of obstacles. When he was a child, he had a goal to ride a bike. Without arms, he couldn't ride a bike in the traditional way, but he and his dad were motivated, resourceful, and strategic, and they fashioned a bike with handlebars that came up to Richie's chest so he could lean forward and steer the bike with his upper body while he pedaled. Certainly, nothing about Richie's life has been easy, but it's an amazing example of how expert learners don't give up, and when they aren't successful in one way, they find another way.

In the video, Richie helps us understand how an expert learner thinks. He says, "There have been people that said that I can't do things, said that I couldn't ride a bicycle, people that said that I couldn't live on my own, couldn't get a good job and support myself, I couldn't go to college and graduate. I don't listen too much to people when they tell me I can't do something. There's not a whole lot that's going to stand in my way."[9]

We need all of our kids to have that same mindset. We need them to know that nothing can stand in their way when they are motivated and encouraged to be resourceful, and when they have the opportunity to do things their way.

When our kids are given choices, they have to take initiative, set goals, and create strategies so they can be successful. This certainly won't happen overnight, but with enough opportunities to practice, students will build these "self-directed" muscles and know that everything they need to be successful is already inside them.

When your kids are little, this self-directed learning will look a lot different than when they are teenagers, but the premise is the same: provide them with options, give them strategies to make decisions and choose options, and then help them build a strategy to meet their goals. If we do that enough, success will come.

When students are self-directed and motivated to learn, they are willing to put forth the effort, take risks, and learn from their mistakes. Now is the time. We are at the beginning of a powerful journey in education where parents and schools come together to create expert learners who are ready to embrace their future. Administrators and teachers want what is best for kids, but sometimes they are committed to outdated pedagogy and policies that prevent the shift to a more personalized education. This is why we have to work together to ensure that all school leaders and teachers know about Universal Design for Learning (UDL), the framework that can make all this happen.

In December 2015, Congress passed the Every Student Succeeds Act (ESSA), which endorses Universal Design for Learning (UDL) as best practice for all students. The UDL framework provides a foundation to teach schools and teachers how to meet the needs of all of our children to activate all three networks of the brain.

When implemented successfully, UDL allows students to make choices that provide them with more ownership of their learning because they can personalize their journey. It's theirs and so it's far more meaningful to them. If we as parents can advocate for UDL, and then support its implementation by incorporating the principles of UDL in our parenting practices, we'll be exactly where we want to be, because our goal of raising successful, happy kids who are always striving for success will have been reached. And not much will stand in their way.

Key Takeaways

- Students learn best when learning opportunities are designed to activate the three networks of the brain that are critical for learning. This is important so students know *why* they are learning, *what* they are learning, and *how* they will use the knowledge or skills in the future.

- All of our kids can become **expert learners**—every single one of them.

- The goal of UDL is not mastery of knowledge; it's about mastery of learning. If we want our kids to be successful, they have to know themselves as learners and know how to reach their goals.

Chapter 3

THE VALUE OF VARIABILITY

Ralph Waldo Emerson, a poet in the Transcendentalist movement in the mid-1800s, wrote, "A foolish consistency is the hobgoblin of little minds....With consistency a great soul has simply nothing to do." He believed that success requires us to be authentic to who we are even if that changes from day to day. Trying to stay the same is, according to Emerson, small-minded. Our kids seem to know that inherently—their interests, moods, and attitudes seem to change by the minute and they don't seem the least concerned by this constant fluctuation. As a parent, it's hard to keep up.

As an example, in the fall, my seven-year-old son Torin woke me up by dragging his feet across my bedroom floor and sighing audibly while donning a white polo shirt.

"Look at me," he said. "I look ridiculous. This shirt is the worst. It's like a dad shirt." Welcome to picture day at the Novak house. The struggle is real. Now, what's important about this story is that the child picked out said polo shirt the weekend before because it was "wicked." I am sure you can all relate.

Instead of arguing, I decided to use this moment as an opportunity for a parenting win, which you have to take when you can get. "You know what, Buddy, you're right. Just dress how you want to dress," I said. He looked skeptical until I added, "I'll talk to Dad."

He ripped off the shirt and disappeared down the hall. I basked in my awesomeness as I brushed my teeth. *I am teaching him to be an individual*, I thought. Emerson, the great poet, would be proud. Who cares if he takes a picture wearing a t-shirt? No big deal. As you all know, savoring parenting glory is always the first mistake.

Ten minutes later, he jumped down the last five stairs and barreled into the kitchen with an Oregon football jersey and florescent green hair, which he spiked with colored hairspray purchased for Halloween. Lots of colored hair-spray. He was holding my hair dryer. "Mom, can you dry this? I need the spikes to go up more." My husband Lon choked on his eggs.

As I tried to perfect his emerald mohawk, he admired himself in the mirror. "My hair is amazing!" I then took this opportunity to provide him with some **mastery-oriented feedback** to help him on his journey to school-picture glory.

"I love that you're so unique. What if maybe you washed out some of that hair spray because when you get older, you might think it's silly you had green hair for your school photo?"

"Why would I think that? It's so awesome."

I tried another tactic. "Well, what about if I let you dye your hair tomorrow instead?"

He wasn't taking the bait. In fact, he gave me my own serving of feedback. "Mom, you do weird things all the time and people like you. This is what I like." Touché.

Let's face the facts. All of our kids are their own person. They differ from us, they differ from each other, and often, they are different from day to day. How many times have you woken up and asked, "Who *is* this kid?"

With four kids of my own, I sometimes feel as though the house is in hostile takeover by complete strangers. Although these constant changes can be frustrating, they are also magical. If we were all the same, life wouldn't be any fun at all.

Allowing our kids the opportunity to chart their course, set their own goals, and reflect on their journey is critical to their success, both at home and in school. Indeed, allowing for and accepting that our children, regardless of

their age, vary from day to day and from one another is an important step we can take as parents to set the stage for them becoming expert learners. Wildly successful adults are expert learners who know what they want and how to get it, honoring all their strengths in the process, and working to overcome their weaknesses. If we want our kids to be happy and successful, we can't define what success looks like for them—only they can. And we have to support them even when their journey takes wild turns, as we know it will. We of course can provide feedback and try to lead them in the right direction, but ultimately, it's their journey.

If we think back to the three networks of the brain, introduced in the second chapter, you'll realize why it's so critical that parents and teachers use multiple strategies to motivate kids, teach them how to access information, and allow them to express what they have learned. And that's really hard to do as a parent because if you have several children, you will no doubt interact with them in different ways. So consider what teachers face when they have a class of upward of 30 students who require slightly different approaches to learning. Traditional education models taught teachers to treat all their students as "one-size-fits-all." But we know now how ineffective and downright disabling that can be—for the teacher and the students.

As a mom, I want all of my kids to be accepted and valued for who they are and I know you want the same. I want them to set their own goals and to follow their own path and like who they are becoming in the process. When my children make choices for themselves, I don't want anyone to see them as different, or as broken. This is especially true when I send them to school.

As an educator, I know a lot about what type of kid schools, teachers, and administrators historically valued. It wasn't second-graders with green hair, students who struggle with or hate reading, kids who cry when they are frustrated in the middle of a test, or students who simply cannot sit still if they are asked to observe their teacher quietly for six hours. Luckily, now educators across the nation are being urged to consider and value **variability**.

A CLOSER LOOK AT VARIABILITY

Variability is the dynamic and ever-changing mix of strengths and challenges that makes up each individual as well as the breadth of differences in any one group (a class of students, for instance). All students have strengths and challenges, which vary widely depending on the learning task. For example, I'm sure you could make a list of ten things you're great at because you have developed an ability or have a natural talent to perform those tasks *already*. On the other hand, you could make an equal list of areas where you haven't developed that ability *yet*.

We need to get to a place in this world where all parents and educators understand that variability is the norm and they celebrate that. Because people are different, they require different experiences in life so they can be successful. Allow me to step back to provide an analogy about variability and shoes.

I love red high heels. They work for me. Now, imagine that I owned the only shoe store in town, and the only thing I sold were red heels (in size 9.5, of course). How would you feel about that? Don't worry if they aren't your size. I can cut out the toe or stuff some tissues in there. Can't walk with heels? I'll teach you, and if I have to, I can saw the heels off. Don't like red? Nothing a little spray paint can't fix. Have an injured foot? Wear them anyway. Don't like them? That's just too bad.

Parenting and teaching are a little like owning a shoe store. As teachers and parents, we all have techniques

One Shoe Fits All?

MY PERFECT SHOE
(IN RED!)

TOO SHORT?
CUT OFF THE TOE!

TOO HIGH?
SAW DOWN THE HEEL

TOO LONG?
STUFF IT WITH TISSUES

that work for us, and we use them repeatedly. We have to remember, however, that they don't always work for our kids, even when we make accommodations and modifications. In the previous example, if I forced you to wear my shoes, it would be like a horrible homage to Cinderella's ugly stepsisters. I can't force one shoe on all of you because there is variability in the size of our shoes, our style, and the level of comfort we require in our footwear, and that changes day to day. You'd want different shoes at the beach than when you're at a wedding because your needs have changed. Variability not only expects these changes, but embraces them.

Because our kids demonstrate variability in any number of ways, they all need a personalized combination of learning experiences in order to succeed. All of these needs can—and should be—addressed in the same classroom. Just as we expect to enter a shoe store and find something perfect for us, so too should our children deserve to enter a classroom with their peers and find something perfect for them. Schools should work toward the goal of creating an education environment where students don't need separate programs to be successful.

When schools don't value variability, they are often prone to fall into what I call the "ability trap," and they create various distinct curriculums and programs for groups of students based on perceived ability. When schools label groups of students, and make assumptions that students can't be educated alongside their peers in inclusive environments, some students may not have the opportunity to develop the skills necessary to self-direct their learning, be creative, and solve problems in collaboration with others.

Because some students are never given the proverbial "10,000 hours" to self-direct and personalize their learning, they may struggle when first given the opportunity to choose learning experiences for themselves, which may be seen as further evidence that a student simply "can't learn." This false and misguided assumption is based on the fallacy of perceived ability, and not on the true potential of an individual student. None of us, not even as parents, know what our kids are capable of accomplishing.

It's important to note that in a universally designed classroom, all student needs are being met. When working with educators and parents on UDL implementation, as I stated previously, people wonder if UDL is really for everyone, especially those students with significant, intensive needs. The answer is yes, and a leader in the field of UDL, Joy Zabala, confirms this. As a technologist, special educator, teacher trainer, and conference speaker, Dr. Zabala has earned international recognition for her work on assistive technology and UDL. According to Dr. Zabala, in an inclusive environment, students with intensive needs may need additional supports or specific assistive technologies that are not available as options for all students, but they can still be provided to students who need them. Assistive technology is critical in these classrooms because it allows students to participate and experience learning with their peers instead of just observing it. Once all students are together in an inclusive environment, teachers can proactively plan learning opportunities using the UDL Guidelines that allow all students the same opportunities to make choices, have a voice, and interact in the classroom.

When kids are segregated in separate classrooms because of perceived ability, they can experience a number of negative outcomes both socially and academically.[10] Socially, students who are not educated with their peers are often excluded because they spend most, if not all, of their day in a different room. As a result, these students are sometimes labeled and stigmatized. Also, academically, students who are educated in small-group settings are often held to lower standards than their peers because teachers often lower the standards as opposed to raising the support and providing additional options.

A universally designed classroom values variability, doesn't focus on perceived ability, and offers different options for all students. In other words, a UDL classroom signals to kids that they are all capable, that all learners have value, and that there are many possible journeys to reach the same destination.

UNIVERSAL DESIGN FOR LEARNING: A FRAMEWORK FOR TEACHING EVERY BRAIN

In 1988, architect Ronald Mace coined the term *Universal Design* and defined it as the "design of products and environments to be useable by all people, to the greatest extent possible, without the need for adaptation or specialized design."[11] Finally, buildings that all people could not enter were called out for what they are: "architecturally disabling." So were parks, sidewalks, and other built environments with barriers built into them. Products that could not be used by those with disabilities were also identified as such.

Think about how empowering that definition is for a moment. People are not disabled. Buildings are. The same is true in classrooms. Not only do schools have to design buildings where all students can enter the building, but they must design curriculum and instruction so all students can experience rigorous, engaging curriculum alongside their peers that is culturally relevant and socially just. When they cannot, it is not the child who is disabled—it is the curriculum.

This concept of creating spaces where all students can be educated, to the greatest extent possible, without the need for adaptation is the foundation of UDL. When schools and teachers universally design learning environments, they are creating more equitable social worlds, just as architects set out to do with universally designed spaces. Since there is no such thing as "average" or "normal," teachers cannot design curriculum and instruction for this mythical student. He or she doesn't exist.

In 1996, CAST (Center for Applied Special Technology), a nonprofit education organization that explored ways to help students with disabilities, coined and defined the concept of *Universal Design for Learning* (UDL), which is the design and delivery of curriculum and instruction to meet the needs of all learners by providing them choices for *why* they are learning, *what* they are learning, and *how* they will share what they have learned in authentic ways. The framework also shifts the focus from the mastery of specific knowledge to the mastery of learning.

To the present day, UDL acknowledges that all students are different and in order to meet their needs, teachers must provide multiple options so that students can personalize their learning. These options provide all students with opportunities to be successful, and therefore school becomes valuable and values everyone. As researchers at CAST have suggested for decades, all students face barriers that prevent them from reaching their full potential in the classroom. Sometimes students face barriers because they don't know, or they don't care, *why* they are learning. Sometimes, they don't understand *what* they are learning, and still other students don't know *how* to express what they have learned. This observation laid the groundwork for the three principles of UDL:

- Provide multiple means of engagement by activating the affective network

- Provide multiple means of representation by activating the recognition network

- Provide multiple means of action and expression by activating the strategic network

These three principles can be applied to the design and delivery of lessons for all students. That way, they can be engaged in learning experiences that meet their needs and allow them to personalize their journey and create their own strategies to master learning goals. The key word here is *all*. Every student deserves the opportunity to be engaged, make choices, and personalize their learning journey.[12]

The UDL Guidelines correspond to the three principles of UDL and help to create expert learners—kids who can set meaningful goals, make meaning with relevant and valuable resources, and share what they know using their own strategies. This results in kids who want to learn and who embrace challenges. The UDL Guidelines are organized according to the three main principles of UDL that address engagement, representation, and action and expression.

Sometimes, when speaking with educators or parents, I am asked, "This sounds innovative and ideal, but I don't think this will work for [those kids]." We can plug a million different types of learners into "those kids." People ask

UDL Guidelines

PROVIDE MULTIPLE MEANS OF

Engagement

Purposeful, motivated learners

Provide options for self-regulation

Provide options for sustaining effort and persistence

Provide options for recruiting interest

PROVIDE MULTIPLE MEANS OF

Representation

Resourceful, knowledgeable learners

Provide options for comprehension

Provide options for language, mathematical expressions, and symbols

Provide options for perception

PROVIDE MULTIPLE MEANS OF

Action & Expression

Strategic, goal-directed learners

Provide options for executive functions

Provide options for expression and communication

Provide options for physical action

about UDL's applicability for students with learning and attention issues; significant, intensive disabilities; social emotional issues; those whose first language is not English, who attend urban schools, who live in poverty, who have significant behavior problems...and the list goes on. My emphatic answer is yes. UDL is for all students. Kids are kids, and they are all different, but they all have the same three networks in their brains, and they all deserve an education that values them as humans, activates those networks, and prepares them for a successful, meaningful future.

In the next section, we'll look at examples of variability in each of the three brain networks. You can begin to consider just how different all of our kids are and how that changes from day to day and why UDL can work for *all* learners.

VARIABILITY IN THE AFFECTIVE NETWORK: THE *WHY*

To achieve something great, we have to establish a meaningful goal, believe it's possible to achieve, and have the ability to cope to overcome all the obstacles that may get in our way. However, often our kids are expected to achieve goals that they didn't have any say in creating, or about which they are not at all interested in achieving. Why should we expect them to feel motivated or persist? At school, teachers often set goals and create strategies for students, which doesn't honor variability in children's affective networks. The same is true at home. When we set goals that are not meaningful or personalized for our kids, it's difficult for them build the necessary commitment and coping strategies to reach those goals.

But all kids will commit when they are striving for their passions. Let's take Walt Disney as an example. Growing up, his father hated that all young Walt wanted to do was draw. He didn't feel there was a future in that, so he forced Walt to take up the fiddle. Disney hated the instrument, was tone deaf, and showed little aptitude, and even less enjoyment, for playing music. That didn't matter to this father, who forced his son to play for an hour a day.[13] Disney rebelled, and eventually, he quit the fiddle to the disappointment of his father. Walt also quit school at the age of sixteen. The Walt Disney we know isn't a quitter. He is a genius. He overcame bankruptcy, multiple failures, and critics who said that he would never amount to anything, that the idea of a large theme park was ridiculous and the idea of a full-length animated film, *Snow White,* nicknamed "Disney's Folly," had no chance of success.[14] Oh, how they were wrong. All Disney needed to be successful was inside him, waiting to flourish, as soon as he was working toward a goal that was meaningful, relevant, and authentic to who he was and who he wanted to become.

Does this mean that teachers and parents should not have goals for kids? No. Teachers are required to teach specific content and skills, and as parents, we work hard to teach our kids to be polite, responsible, kind, and diligent. The issue is that often we fail to consider that there are many ways to personalize a goal to make the outcome more relevant and meaningful to the individual child. For example, we may have a goal that all of our kids write thank-you cards after receiving a gift or kindness. When we step back, the goal is really that our kids are thankful and appreciative, isn't it? It may be far more personal and meaningful for them to thank someone in person with a hug, or call to share a conversation over the phone, so why are we insisting on a handwritten note? Allowing students the opportunity to make a goal relevant and meaningful is the key to personalization.

The same is true in all learning environments. Teachers may set a goal that all students become strong readers. To achieve this goal, they may assign the same text to the entire class. Instead, providing students with an option to read about what they want in a format that is meaningful gets students' attention. In the same class, one student could be reading an ESPN magazine; others could be sitting at a table together poring over the latest issue of *The New York Times*. In the same class, another student could listen to an audiobook on his IPhone while a classmate pages through a traditional novel, highlighting text as she reads. In this example, all students are building important skills in reading comprehension, but they have set more personalized goals to challenge themselves with content that speaks to them. The variability in their goals helps them develop personalized strategies, techniques, and coping skills to achieve what is meaningful to them.

Getting students' attention and supporting them as they create meaningful goals is only the beginning. They also must build the skills to self-regulate and cope because goals worth achieving are usually those that are just a little out of our reach. Indeed, one way we can define success is pushing beyond boundaries to accomplish something great. In our previous example, we don't want students to pick text that is a breeze to read. Instead, we want them to self-reflect and pick something challenging, because comprehending challenging text is like solving a puzzle— it requires mental effort and work, which is exactly how learners become stronger at critical thinking.

Unfortunately, there is no magic formula to provide our kids with motivation, grit, and resilience due to the natural variability in the affective network. To overcome obstacles, our kids have to be presented with multiple options so they can try some, fail, reflect, and eventually learn what works best for them as they struggle.

In the book *Mind Over Matter: The Surprising Power of Expectations*, education journalist Chris Berdik discusses how some athletes are able to push boundaries, break world records, and play under pressure, whereas other athletes "choke." Although he doesn't discuss UDL explicitly, it's clear that "choking" occurs in the affective network and athletes who can overcome "choking" can do that because they have developed effective self-regulation and coping strategies that work for them.[15]

Think of a situation when your child was expected to do something challenging: maybe it was reading a challenging text or solving a difficult math problem; competing in an athletic event, a dance recital, or math competition; or preparing for an upcoming standardized test. If the task is challenging, your child probably felt nervous, anxious, or frustrated, which would be completely natural. As parents, we often swoop in to help to calm them so they don't "choke" or get more upset. The problem is, we probably provide a "one-size-fits-all," approach to de-stressing. However, the tried-and-true strategies that are effective for us may not be the best ones for our kids. As psychologist Stuart Shanker says, "All too often we confuse our needs with the child's. We seek to make children more manageable, rather than self-managing."[16]

Instead, we might try to offer advice like, "Take a deep breath. Slow down and focus," but that won't work for every child. Interestingly, taking it slow and calming down helps some, whereas it actually hurts others because the hyper focus on calming down becomes the primary goal, and performance and success become the secondary goal.

It's also important to note that asking kids to calm down may actually trigger frustration. They don't know what it feels like to calm down, they are uncomfortable with the feeling of being calm because their lives are so fast-paced, or they find slower paced activities boring. This is why we, as parents and teachers, have to offer multiple options for being calm.

Trying to distract a child, as a way to help them to cope and manage stress, can also backfire. Counting backward, or singing a song, may help some kids self-regulate so they are able to continue while working toward a task, but it may also divert their attention. Learners who try to concentrate on too many things at once can be referred to as *cognitively busy*. The state of being cognitively busy has the potential to weaken performance and increase distraction because when you force yourself to do something (like count backward), you are expending mental work so you have far less energy to persist on the challenging task at hand.[17]

Another possible technique outlined in Berdik's *Mind Over Matter* for building self-regulation is to increase anxiety in practice and in other situations. Doing so will allow kids to get more comfortable with the feeling of being uncomfortable. That technique, in particular, probably makes many of you uncomfortable just thinking about it—but many successful athletes use this strategy regularly to get accustomed to performing under pressure.

Because of variability in the affective network, our kids will develop very different strategies to self-regulate under pressure as they attempt to work toward challenging goals and focus on *why* they must persist to achieve their goal. We, as parents, won't know which one is the most effective until our kids try and fail and then experience success. This requires us to share multiple options and encourage our kids to try them—you want your kids to learn to fail!

Learning and achieving success both require options. Providing kids with only one path to success more than likely will leave many of them at a dead end. But letting them understand that there are always countless other roads, and one of them is going to lead to success, will enable each of our kids to succeed.

The first step, however, is for students to know the ultimate destination and why it's important to reach it. In each course, there are outcomes, or standards, that students work to achieve. The means for reaching this goal may vary.

In English/language arts, for example, it's important that students learn how to determine an author's purpose in a text and analyze how an author uses rhetoric to advance that purpose. When students develop this skill, they have the tools to think critically about a message, unpack the techniques the author is using, and determine if there is a hidden agenda, before they decide if they are going to be persuaded to think or act in a certain way. This understanding, which is useful and authentic for all learners, is the lesson's goal.

This destination can be explained at the beginning of each lesson so that if an observer were to walk into a classroom and say to a student, "Why are you working on this? What is the goal?" they would be able to answer. (Note: An appropriate answer is not "Because the teacher told us to.")

In this scenario, in a universally designed lesson, students would be given the option to learn about different rhetorical strategies through a class presentation, course readings, or a teacher presentation. They could then choose a text to analyze—it could be a famous speech, an advertisement in a magazine, a political campaign, social media posts, or an infomercial. This would provide them with an opportunity to personalize their journey to analyze an author's purpose in a meaningful, authentic way. Students could also have an option to express their rhetorical analysis in many different ways. Some students may write a blog; others may pen a letter to the author, or give a class presentation. In this example, the ultimate destination is clear, but there are many roads to get there.

Let's examine another example from the classroom of how a teacher makes the goal of the lesson really clear, and then provides all students with options. This time, we'll visit a hypothetical first-grade class, so you can imagine how even our youngest learners can be self-directed and creative when they are working toward a specific goal.

Imagine a first-grade teacher sitting in a rocking chair at Circle Time. The teacher opens the book *Kindness Is Cooler, Mrs. Ruler*,[18] and starts with *why*.

> Today, we are going to read books about being kind. As a school we have been preparing for World Kindness Day. We are going to start with this book, so we can talk about kindness, and then you will choose your own book about kindness.
>
> This book may be challenging, but since you are all super-readers and never give up, you will be able to read all about how Mrs. Ruler's class learns to be kind. You will have a couple of choices for reading. You can read it by yourself or with a small group, you can read it while listening to it on the headphones, or you can sit with me and I will read it to you. It doesn't matter what anyone else picks. You choose what it best for you, and don't worry—you can change your mind.
>
> For example, if you try to read by yourself, remember our tricks about "just right books." Can anyone tell me how you can tell if a book is just right? […] That's right. If there are three words on a page that you can't read, you may want to change your strategy. Can someone remind me what a strategy is?

In this example, it's clear that the teacher values all learners, regardless of variability, and although the students will make different choices, they will all arrive at the same goal. If you imagine your child as a first-grader in that scenario, you can probably guess what he or she would pick. The magic is the choice!

After the students make their choices, the teacher may provide students with choices to get comfortable so they can dive into the story. She may say:

> You can read at your desk, sit on the floor, or come over here with me. Feel free to enjoy your snack if you wish. In ten minutes, we'll do a quick check-in to see how we're feeling and change our strategies if necessary. After that, you will get to choose your own book about kindness from our library collection or from your Raz-kids online account on the IPad, and we will make connections. When we are done, you will share an example of kindness from your book in writing, by drawing a picture, or by telling the class.

In this example, while focusing on the *why*, the teacher builds engagement by giving students choices, minimizes threats and distractions, encourages students to set their own goals, promotes expectations that optimize motivation, and facilitates personal coping skills.

Note in this example how the students are empowered through engagement. The teacher did not assign students to groups based on reading levels. She encouraged autonomy, and she challenged them to define their own action steps and coping strategies, all while creating a motivating, warm environment, one where expert learners can grow.

VARIABILITY IN THE RECOGNITION NETWORK, THE *WHAT*

Our kids aren't only different in how their interest is recruited and how they self-regulate under pressure, but they also differ in how they perceive information. One extreme example of this variability in the recognition network is the neurologic disorder, prosopagnosia. Sometimes referred to as face blindness, prosopagnosia affects about 2 percent of the population.[19] Children and adults with prosopagnosia cannot identify a person by their face or facial features. When they look at someone, they may notice details like earrings or a hairstyle, but they can't holistically process a face and identify a person that way.

In 2012, David Roger Fine, a 60-year-old physician with lifelong face blindness, reflected on his childhood and his inability to process faces: "I can remember the building and its surroundings in almost photographic detail, but no faces. If I think of the headmistress, I see sandy red hair and freckles, but no face. If I think of three boys I was friendly with, I remember that one had a battered hand-me-down cap, another brogue shoes, the third glasses with an eye blanked out to treat a 'lazy eye,' but no faces."[20] Although the disorder is rare, this admittedly extreme example demonstrates just how complex recognition can be, and it is not always a matter of preference. Recognizing information isn't only about access. Indeed, sometimes students have preferences that allow them to make meaning much more effectively, given their particular strengths, weaknesses, or combination thereof. A good example of how any one person's skills combine to impact their ability to recognize and understand information can be seen through the lens of the theory of multiple intelligences. Howard Gardner, a renowned professor at Harvard University, proposed eight different types of intelligences because "intelligence" is far too limiting a concept.[21]

The eight intelligences are illustrated here:

You may have a child who struggles on traditional assessments but is incredibly empathetic and is able to connect with people. Being "people smart" is a talent that should continue to be fostered and valued, but schools do not always value all intelligences equally. Dr. Gardner notes that schools traditionally value students who are "word smart" and "number/reasoning smart," and when students struggle in these areas, they are identified as being learning disabled. But it's not learners who are disabled. Curriculum and instruction are disabled when they don't provide students with opportunities to personalize their journey so they can maximize their strengths and find their own meaning of success.

Dr. Gardner's theory on the importance of multiple intelligences speaks directly to the importance of teachers using options to meet the needs of all learners. He urges all teachers to individualize and pluralize. His definition of individualizing is when educators teach and assess in ways that bring out each child's capabilities. This is not possible without providing options, because variability is so significant. Pluralizing speaks to importance of providing options to reach more students because multiple modes of delivery allow students to thoroughly understand topics as they can think about them in many different ways.

Another example of how our kids perceive and recognize information differently is through their love languages. The love languages were identified by Gary Chapman, a world-renowned marriage counselor whose work on love languages has helped countless couples appreciate the variability in how the other communicates love. After working with couples, Dr. Chapman realized that the lessons were equally applicable to adult/child relationships. The five love languages impact whether or not our kids perceive the love we're trying to give them, or whether they feel like they are truly valued by the adults in their lives, including their teachers. Short descriptions of the five love languages follow with implications for parenting, teaching, and learning. If you're interested in taking a short quiz to identify your love language or the love language of your kids, visit *www.5lovelanguages.com*.

Words of Affirmation   The first love language is words of affirmation. These are the kids who need praise and appreciation to feel motivated and loved. We may try to show our kids love by attending every school function and athletic event and hugging and kissing them every night before bed, but if you have a child whose primary love language is words of affirmation, that may not be enough. These kids thrive on compliments, handwritten notes in their lunch boxes, and text messages. In school, their teachers need to praise their effort, write detailed feedback on their papers, and acknowledge their strengths and all the great things that make them unique so they feel valued for who they are.

Acts of Service   Some kids thrive on acts of service. These are the kids who would prefer that you do something for them, to take something off their plate. At home, they are often asking for help cleaning their rooms, fixing their bikes, or revising their homework. In classrooms, they are often asking teachers for help on projects and assignments, not because they can't do it alone, but because they feel valued when teachers are willing to help.

Gifts   If your child is into gifts, it's pretty self-explanatory. You can inspire anything, from a clean room to straight A's, with the promise of new sneakers, professional highlights, the newest iPhone, or a Lightning McQueen car. In school, teachers can motivate students with the promise of a donut party, a homework pass, a jar full of Jolly Ranchers, new pencils, or a token from a classroom store or prize box.

Quality Time   Some kids thrive on quality time. They want to sit and play board games, have you practice shooting hoops with them, and sit next to them while they are completing their homework, no matter how old they are. In school, they feel valued when teachers take the time to sit next to their desk and have a conversation, ask about their day, and take the time to meet with them before or after school for extra help. These kids can be motivated by the promise of an extra recess or lunch with their favorite teacher.

Physical Touch   Finally, you have your physical touch kids, your snugglers. They want shoulder rubs, hugs, and they love to hold your hand. This "safe touch" is critical for some students, and yet their needs may not be met because of recent "no-touch" policies in school. Teacher and mother Jessica Lahey, the author of the bestseller *A Gift of Failure*, wrote an article in *The Atlantic* titled "Should Teachers Be Allowed to Touch Students?"[22] The article examines the importance of "safe touch" for some students. Lahey wrote, "Every child is different, with varying needs for social touch. Some children, such as those on the autism spectrum, may have a much lower need for touch, while other children may require frequent, close contact." As with everything in UDL, it's critical that teachers have the power to provide students with the option to get what they need to feel valued, appreciated, and loved.

Love languages are an example of how our kids recognize efforts to communicate in very different ways. One size doesn't fit all when it comes to the *what* of learning, and so teaching and learning become even more nuanced as teachers consider how to teach students while also showing them they are valued in ways they can recognize. Kids can have combos, with one that is dominant.

If teachers fully embrace the fact that no two individuals have the same mix of strengths and weaknesses, they will then be more motivated to provide a class of students with options so the students themselves can begin to personalize their learning by making choices. They will intuitively choose to learn from resources that make the most sense to their unique mix of intelligences and build upon their own strengths.

Because of student variability, all teachers need to get to know students, their strengths and weaknesses, and what makes them unique. Once they understand the range of variability in any given group of students, teachers can then provide multiple representations that allow all of our kids to access information in many different ways.

Traditional teaching has relied heavily on reading text and listening to teacher lectures, but not every child can understand or make meaning from the same book or lecture simply because that's not the best way for them to learn. For example, a student with a hearing impairment will be at a disadvantage if a teacher relies on lectures as the sole presentation of content. A student with a deficit in working memory or a difference in background knowledge might also miss a learning opportunity because they struggle to keep up with the verbal presentation of the teacher, who is using vocabulary unfamiliar to the student. If a student has attention issues, a lecture is difficult to comprehend because there is no option to rewind and watch again.

However, when teachers offer students different representations of information—lecture, slides, notes on the board, access to video files, for example—students become more motivated and engaged. They might choose to access visuals, work in small groups to learn information, view demonstrations in class or online, watch videos, read books or online text, or listen to audio. They also may have opportunities to use their devices to access information, which offers them tools to support their recognition of vocabulary and complex concepts. Students can look up the meaning of difficult words, ask questions of their peers in classroom blogs, and research reputable sites or use apps to help build background knowledge. The options are endless when teachers put students in the driver's seat and encourage them to figure out how to meet the end goals of any given assignment. In this way, teachers and students become partners in the design of their learning experience.

VARIABILITY IN THE STRATEGIC NETWORK

Our kids differ not only in how they cope when presented with challenges (affective network) and how they recognize information and perceive that they are valued (recognition network), but they also vary in how they plan, organize, and initiate actions (the strategic network).

You can see such variability in the strategies the competitors for the Scripps National Spelling Bee use to memorize the spelling of an immerse list of words. Scripps is the Super Bowl of spelling bees, televised every year by ESPN and viewed by millions. Kids between the ages of six and fifteen are thrust on a national stage as they attempt to spell words like Feldenkrais and prestidigitation.

The movie *Spellbound*, nominated for an Academy Award in 2002 for best documentary, followed eight competitors for the Scripps National Spelling Bee in an effort to understand how ordinary kids can become such expert spellers. The eight kids had markedly different strategies for learning to spell. For example, a young girl, Nupur, sat on the couch each night while her mother quizzed her from the dictionary, moving slowly from the beginning to the end. Ashley, a student in the Washington D.C. Public Schools, stayed after school every day to study with her teacher. The teacher supported Ashley by turning spelling into various games, instead of repetitive practice or "drill and kill" methods. For example, in one scene in the documentary the teacher encourages Ashley to open up the dictionary to a random page. From there, the teacher read the words and Ashley used Scrabble tiles to spell them.

Neil studied from a list of all the words compiled from the data from all previous Scripps Spelling Bees. He studied between 7,000 and 8,000 words a day with this father. He also worked with a spelling coach Monday–Thursday, three hours a day. On Saturday, he worked with his spelling coach for four to eight hours. He also had a French teacher, a Spanish teacher, and a German teacher who provided tutoring to help him learn the words with particular origins.

While these students all have the same goal—being the best speller they can be—the strategies by which they reach that goal and express their knowledge of the words they are expected to spell are completely individual, demonstrating the extreme variability in the strategic network of the brain.

We cannot expect students to express their understanding in just one way. Two popular methods to assess students are written responses and objective multiple-choice tests. There are countless barriers to each of these assessments. For example, when a student is asked to write a paper, they may struggle because they lack a writing utensil or don't have access to technology to keyboard a response; they may have poor handwriting or keyboarding skills; or they may struggle with format, spelling, grammar, or communication. Now, no one would argue that being able to communicate is important, but requiring all content to be expressed in a written response is limiting. If the purpose of the assessment is to measure knowledge, and not writing, then there are plenty of options for students to share what they have learned, even if they lack a pen or haven't learned how to organize a paper *yet*.

Imagine that your son or daughter struggles with written expression. Now, imagine that a high school history teacher asks students to analyze the Declaration of Independence, either by reading the text or listening to an audio version, and then he provides students with the option to communicate the major themes of the document in an essay, or a series of political cartoons, a class debate, an online podcast, or a multimedia presentation. Think about how much more engaged and successful all our kids would be if these options were available to them.

Now, this may give you pause because there is a nagging question: "How will students ever learn to write an essay if they can choose *not* to?" The answer kicks back to the affective network and why the assessment is being assigned. If the assessment is designed to measure students' knowledge of the Declaration of Independence, writing is not the *why*. It's not the goal. If, in fact, writing is the goal, and teachers need all students to learn how to organize and write informative text, then they need a universally designed lesson on *why* essay writing is important, *what* a solid essay includes, and *how* to write one. In the spirit of options, they should be provided with exemplars, graphic organizers, checklists, and the ability to write about something they are passionate about. Also, to ensure that they can monitor their progress, reflect, and improve their writing, it's important that teachers provide lots of feedback while students are working, as well as opportunities to revise and strategies to help them cope with frustration. The affective network is always at play in the background, monitoring learning and coping with setbacks so the learner can sustain effort and persistence. Small options go a long way, such as the option for students to listen to music on their devices while they work, chew gum or enjoy mints, have a quick mindfulness break, or work at a standing desk or sit in a comfortable chair.

At home, we can use the knowledge of this variability to help our kids attain their goals. Take, for example, the simple request of "Clean your room." The goal is clear enough, but all kids will vary widely in how they complete this task (if of course, you can first get them motivated enough to start!).

Think for a second about what you expect when you ask your kids to clean their rooms. In my fantasy world, I actually expect the bed to be made, clothes to be folded and put away, toys and electronics to be stored, and the floor to be swept, in that order. In reality, what happens is that everything is shoved under the bed and in the closet and then the bed is made and the floor is half swept. And I am ripping mad! But why? When I walk in, the room is "clean." So, if we want our kids to activate their strategic network, we need to let them do things their way or we need to provide them with supports so they know exactly what they need to include in their strategy. The magic is making the goal crystal clear and allowing them to recognize exactly what is expected, so they can find a way to do it on their own. Just as UDL requires teachers to become partners with students in achieving goals, so too can we become partners with our kids.

Because the three networks of the brain work together in a system, our kids can't isolate the strategic network to get their room clean. Instead, we first have to provide them with a valuable reason why they need to clean the room and/or we have to motivate them to do that. If you ask your son or daughter to clean their room, for example, and their response is, "Why?" it's time for a conversation about the importance of the goal. Although you may cringe to think about sitting down to discuss whether it's appropriate for a child to clean his room, consider the power of opening up the dialogue and asking them to self-reflect. You may start with, "You know what? I'm interested in your perspective. Why don't you tell me why you think it's important to have a messy room?" You never know where the conversation will lead. Allowing them to share their ideas shows that you value where they are coming from. From there, you can provide feedback to help them understand why cleanliness is important. For example, after Halloween, my boys ended up with bunches of candy wrappers under their bed and a trail of mouse poop. Once I pointed this out, it was an easy sell to motivate them to clean up those wrappers and never bring food into their room again. Having the visual of the mouse droppings certainly activated both their affective networks and their recognition networks and from there, they were very goal-directed. My oldest son even asked me to create a checklist of everything that should be done when cleaning the room. All three networks came together on that one!

These examples highlight the significant variability in our kids and how many options are necessary to meet all their needs. Now imagine what our teachers are up against. If they want to create a learning environment where all our kids are successful, they have to consider the significant variability of their class as they design every lesson. That way, all of our kids can feel motivated and valued, and have opportunities to make choices that make learning relevant, accessible, and strategic.

School leaders, teachers, and parents who think about and then adopt a universally designed approach to teaching and learning will enable so many more students to experience success in school. When all involved consider the variability of students in any classroom, and actively deploy a proven strategy to reach all learners, then the "achievement gap" between certain populations of students will begin to close. This gap exists in part because not enough care is paid to variability and diversity in the *design* of classroom instruction. UDL offers a straightforward and accessible way to remedy this.

Kids who don't know how to become expert learners are frustrated, bored, defiant, or rebellious, and they may not be able to succeed on achievement measures. They may not want to go to school, or they may fail assessments, but that's not because they aren't capable of learning. All students are capable of expert learning and success if we as parents can partner with schools to help push the use of UDL in the classroom and support our kids at home using the same strategies. By doing so, we will ensure that all our kids experience the same opportunities to succeed in today's classrooms.

Key Takeaways

- Variability is the norm. Because all our children are different, they require different learning experiences to be successful.

- UDL is focused on the variability of students and not just their ability. All kids have a mix of strengths and weaknesses, and we should celebrate that and not use those differences to label students.

Chapter 4

WHY CHOICE ISN'T JUST NICE, IT'S NECESSARY

I hope by now that you can see how Universal Design for Learning (UDL) is, at its core, a framework for learning that values all kids and their variability. But the question is, how do you go about applying the principles of UDL so everyone can personalize their experience and get what they need? Specifically, you may be wondering how a teacher would begin to incorporate UDL as he or she designs and delivers curriculum and instruction. Although we'll get to that, it's important for you to experience the power of incorporating UDL into something as simple as a nice summer cookout.

For me, nothing beats a cookout for starting summer off on the right note. There's something about the warm summer air that makes friends and family break out their coolers, fire up the charcoal grill, play loud music, and stay outside until all hours of the night. Regardless of where you live in the nation, the traditional cookout is a summer tradition that we all share. Most cookouts include hamburgers and hot dogs, bags of chips, macaroni or potato salad, and sliced watermelon. In rows of coolers, hosts bury cans of soda and beer in ice. Entertainment is also predictable—bocce, horseshoes, or maybe a pickup game of volleyball. This traditional cookout works for so many guests, which is why it has become a go-to pastime of summer and friendship.

But take a minute to think about a cookout from this new lens of variability: perhaps a cookout might not work for everyone. Let me share a story. Last summer, my husband and I were in the midst of planning for a cookout for

our son's lacrosse team. The conversation went something like this:

> *"Hey, we should probably get a menu together since we're going to have over 40 people over on Saturday."*
>
> *"We'll be fine if we just do burgers, dogs, and chips and then we can pick up some beers."*

After that, we discussed entertainment—the typical sprinkler, lacrosse scrimmage, fire pit routine—and figured we had a pretty nice little party planned.

Here's the spoiler alert: the party that we planned is not designed to meet the needs of everyone in attendance because we didn't use the principles of Universal Design for Learning or consider the variability of our guests. Granted, most kids and their families would be psyched about a cheeseburger and a beer, but what about the guests who might be vegetarian? Or vegan? Or gluten-intolerant? What about the guests who had severe allergies to corn or peanut butter?

Since we had invited all the families from our son's team, there were plenty of people we didn't know well. Suddenly, I realized that UDL principles actually applied to this situation. To be ready for any type of eater, we needed to offer a range of food options, making sure everyone could find at least one food to enjoy.

So I turned to my husband and said, "That's an awesome start, but what if someone doesn't want burgers or if someone is trying to eat healthy? Just pick up some chicken, veggies, and hummus. I think Costco also has some veggie burgers that are good. We need more options for everyone."

"Yeah. Good point. Let's make a salad too and cut up some fruit."

In this UDL cookout, my husband and I were anticipating the variability of our guests and planned to have a buffet of options for them. Notice we didn't have to label any of our guests. In our planning, we ensured that we have something for everyone, not just "the vegetarian" and "the friend on Weight Watchers," but any guest who arrives, ready to party.

If you value variability, then it makes sense to plan a UDL cookout. Once your guests arrive, you can empower them to make decisions for themselves so they can enjoy some delicious food and feel welcomed. Put out all the different dishes on the counter, provide everyone with the tools they need to serve, and then allow everyone to dive in.

You may realize from this analogy that the different options don't benefit just those guests who could not consume the original menu of chips and burgers. I am not

a vegetarian, but I'd love a plate piled high with grilled zucchini and salad.

If we continue to explore our cookout analogy, you can see why self-reflection is so critical in helping students build self-direction. If our kids head straight to the Sprite cooler and the brownie table, we would definitely check in with them to ask them about their goal and whether they were making the best decision for themselves. This collaboration is critical because it helps both parties understand each other better. Also, it gives kids a voice. Maybe they already ate a whole plate of chicken and veggies, and we somehow missed it. Maybe they didn't know where to find the zucchini and mushrooms and figured, "Hey, I'll just settle for brownies." (Hey, it could happen!). You'll never know about their goal or their strategy until you reach out to interact and get feedback to understand how you might help them get back on track, if necessary. In this scenario, when we provide the buffet, we fully realize that all of our guests may not be able to make a healthy plate *yet*. In UDL, we value mistakes for their potential to teach something new.

Next, I'll describe the UDL Guidelines, with our "cookout" translations. As you review the translations, imagine how these Guidelines would encourage all your guests to create a personalized party experience without you worrying about each individual guest's needs. The goal of these Guidelines would be to help set the stage that all your guests can feel like "expert guests"— friends and acquaintances who are excited to attend the party and have fun. All will benefit from increased enjoyment because they will discover plenty of options that satisfy them.

PROVIDE MULTIPLE MEANS OF ENGAGEMENT

When your guests are invited to your party, you want to get their attention so they know that your cookout will be an awesome time. You can share some of the reasons why the party will be so awesome as soon as you send out that Evite, text message, and/or Facebook invitation. As we discussed previously, getting someone's attention and interest is the easy part; keeping it is more challenging. As you consider the Guidelines for engagement, you also have to think about how you're going to keep them entertained throughout the whole party. Also, never underestimate the importance of disaster relief. What happens if it rains? What if you run out of propane? A universally designed party planner always expects the unexpected!

All the work you do get everyone psyched about your party before, during, and after is how you're going to activate the affective network. The following table provides you with some considerations so that your party meets the needs of all of your guests as you provide options for recruiting interest, options for sustaining effort and persistence, and options for self-regulation.

Summer Kickoff BBQ

MAY 19

2PM - 8PM

**"COME ONE, COME ALL!
COME LATE...COME EARLY!"**

Dress Code

SPORT COAT   HOODIE   PARTY DRESS

Wear what you'd like as long as you are comfy.

Food & Drink

We'll have beer, wine and soda, burgers (meat & veggie), chicken, mac & cheese, salads and more.

Activities

CARD GAMES   CRAFTS   FIRE PIT   LAWN GAMES

Text or call Katie by May 16 to RSVP (555-333-1234

Guidelines for the Principle of Multiple Means of Engagement

PROVIDE MULTIPLE MEANS OF ENGAGEMENT	HOW YOU'D USE THE GUIDELINES FOR PARTY PLANNING
Provide options for self-regulation: ■ Promote expectations and beliefs that optimize motivation ■ Facilitate personal coping skills and strategies ■ Develop self-assessment and reflection	■ Offer options to guests so any hesitation they have about attending the party are minimized. Make it clear that arriving late or leaving early is perfectly acceptable, that they can wear whatever they want, and although they are welcome to bring a dish or drink, it's not required. ■ Prevent guests from getting bored or anxious by providing options for entertainment like horseshoes, a deck of cards, sidewalk chalk for the kids, and so forth. You can also have a quiet area to get away from the action, like a room with a football game on, or a fire pit.
Provide options for sustaining effort and persistence: ■ Heighten salience of goals and objectives ■ Vary demands and resources to optimize challenge ■ Foster collaboration and communication ■ Increase mastery-oriented feedback	■ Is it for a birthday celebration? End-of the year party or just a chance to connect? If you're having a Halloween party, are costumes encouraged? Make sure the goal of the party is clear so everyone is prepared. ■ Encourage guests to ride-share or bring their kids. During the party, introduce guests to one another and let them know what they have in common. Also, you can have the option for team games like bocce, Pictionary, or tug-o-war. ■ Consistently check in with guests to provide options to maximize their experience.

PROVIDE MULTIPLE MEANS OF ENGAGEMENT	HOW YOU'D USE THE GUIDELINES FOR PARTY PLANNING
Provide options for recruiting interest: ■ Optimize individual choice and autonomy ■ Optimize relevance, value, and authenticity ■ Minimize threats and distractions	■ Let guests know there will be countless options at the party for them to personalize their experience—the food, the entertainment (i.e., options to watch the game, go swimming, play board games, roast marshmallows), whether they want to bring kids, and so forth. ■ Share the message that you want people to come as they are (i.e., "If you'd like to bring a special dish or drink, please feel free!" or "No dress code—just wear whatever you'd like!").

Provide Multiple Means of Representation

Hopefully your invitation is recruiting interest, but in order to do that, the message has to be received by everyone. In today's world, we can't just send out an invitation in one way. If you've ever tried an Evite, you know that there are always a handful of guests who never open the invitation. Also, when guests arrive, do they understand house rules? How will they know about them? The following Guidelines will help to build knowledge in all your guests.

Guidelines for the Principle of Multiple Means of Representation

PROVIDE MULTIPLE MEANS OF REPRESENTATION	HOW YOU'D USE THE GUIDELINES FOR PARTY PLANNING
Provide options for perception: ▪ Offer ways of customizing the display of information ▪ Offer alternatives for auditory information ▪ Offer alternatives for visual information	▪ Send out an electronic invitation, but also send out a text, Facebook invite, handwritten invitation, and/or make a phone call if necessary.
Provide options for language, mathematical expressions, and symbols: ▪ Clarify vocabulary and symbols ▪ Clarify syntax and structure ▪ Support decoding of text, mathematical notation, and symbols ▪ Promote understanding across languages ▪ Illustrate through multiple media	▪ Provide QR codes with recipes so guests can scan and check for allergens, nutrition information, etc. ▪ Include visuals if you have important house instructions; don't just post written directions. Signs incorporate text and visuals to ensure that your guests are clear on your expectations.

PROVIDE MULTIPLE MEANS OF REPRESENTATION	HOW YOU'D USE THE GUIDELINES FOR PARTY PLANNING
Provide options for comprehension: ■ Activate or supply background knowledge ■ Highlight patterns, critical features, big ideas, and relationships ■ Guide information processing, visualization, and manipulation ■ Maximize generalization and transfer	■ Post photos of past parties so guests know what to expect, and post pictures of your house or put out balloons so everyone can find it. ■ Highlight the who, what, where, and why on the party invitation and send reminders. ■ Highlight parking directions, insert links to maps, etc.

Provide Multiple Means of Action and Expression

You also want to make sure that everyone is able to achieve their goal of having a blast at the cookout of the year, but because of the significant variability of your guests, you have to make sure you offer multiple options for physical action, and for how they will create a strategy so they are having a blast. The UDL Guidelines for Action and Expression will help you offer different levels of activity and optimize choice throughout the whole experience.

Guidelines for the Principle of Multiple Means of Action and Expression

PROVIDE MULTIPLE MEANS OF ACTION AND EXPRESSION	HOW YOU'D USE THE GUIDELINES FOR PARTY PLANNING
Provide options for physical action: ■ Vary the methods for response and navigation ■ Optimize access to tools and assistive technologies	■ Ensure that there is an entrance to the party area that is accessible even if guests are on crutches or struggle with mobility issues. ■ Provide different seating arrangements like tray tables, dining table seating, and signs to encourage guests to eat on couches, outside, etc.
Provide options for expression and communication: ■ Use multiple media for communication ■ Use multiple tools for construction and composition ■ Build fluencies with graduated levels of support for practice and performance	■ When you send out the invitation, allow guests to RSVP by calling, emailing, texting, or using an Evite. ■ Provide different utensils—forks, spoons, and chopsticks; straws for drinking; and different sizes of plates and napkins. ■ Provide an extra basket of beach towels, some bug spray, and some extra sweatshirts that guests can grab if they need them.

PROVIDE MULTIPLE MEANS OF ACTION AND EXPRESSION	HOW YOU'D USE THE GUIDELINES FOR PARTY PLANNING
Provide options for executive functions: ■ Guide appropriate goal-setting ■ Support planning and strategy development ■ Facilitate managing information and resources ■ Enhance capacity for monitoring progress	■ When you invite guests, share some tips for preparing for, and arriving at the party—providing directions and the hours of the party allows everyone to make a plan. ■ When you send the invite, provide guests with tips so they have everything they need for the party (BYOB? Bring sweatshirt? Be ready for board games?). ■ During the party, ask guests if they need anything, or if there's anything you can provide to make the party more fun.

Considering the UDL party planning guidelines helps you create a party where your guests feel valued, empowered to enjoy the party in whatever way they wish, and have very personalized experiences while also still RSVPing, "Yes!" despite their variability.

How does this cookout analogy point to ways in which teachers might begin to use the Guidelines to proactively plan lessons that empower students to become agents in the design and delivery of their education? In the next chapter, we will examine why some of the nation's teachers are not yet ready, willing, and able to implement UDL in their classrooms and schools. Then, we will take a look at what would need to happen in order to eliminate those barriers so that all of our kids have the benefit of an engaging, personalized experience that values them as individuals, while also giving them what they need to succeed in the future.

Key Takeaways

- The UDL Guidelines provide the blueprint for a universally designed experience.

- A universally designed cookout will meet the needs of all your guests without you having to plan individual experiences or make accommodations. This analogy will help you consider how teachers can use the UDL Guidelines to design experiences for students that allow them to personalize their learning.

Chapter 5

WHAT TEACHERS ARE UP AGAINST

*A*sking schools and teachers to turn away from traditional practices is asking them to walk into uncharted territory. Trying something new can be scary because it requires vulnerability and effort and there are no guarantees that success will happen right away. However, even though change is always challenging, it is necessary. Yes—the traditional education model has been effective for some students, but it is not designed to be effective for all students, especially in our world today.

Education has changed tremendously since we were in school, and that's a good thing for our kids and for our world. All the differences that we used to call disabilities, quirks, or behavior problems are now just a part of the human variability, and educators across the country are being urged to see students and value them for who they are. In short, many schools have to change. But change is hard—especially when there are so many things that are changing at once.

Knowing what teachers are up against may help to provide a rationale for why UDL is not being implemented as quickly as we would like it to be.

TIME IS STRETCHED TOO THIN

Teachers sometimes have low expectations for themselves and their students because they struggle with feelings of efficacy. Teacher efficacy refers to a teacher's belief about the extent to which students' learning can be influenced by their teaching. In general, teachers who believe that they can positively influence student outcomes are more likely to provide all students with the support and the opportunities they need to succeed.

When teachers have a high sense of efficacy, they become expert learners who help students to set more challenging goals, and they persist despite obstacles to student learning.[23] Teacher efficacy consistently predicts student achievement, even when student variability is statistically controlled—which is why it's so critical to provide all teachers with quality professional development in UDL so they can begin to see, and believe, that student learning is within their control.[24] Unfortunately, professional development resources are often spread too thin and teachers can't get what they need to see how UDL would be effective in their learning environments.

When I work with educators around the world, the biggest barriers I hear for why schools aren't implementing UDL is "Initiative overload" and "There's not enough time."

Schools have so many initiatives on their plates that ask teachers to change what they do or how they do things, and there is not enough time to spend quality time on all of them. As a result, professional development is often scattered, spending only a few hours on one topic before moving on. This spread-too-thin approach to professional development contributes to the teacher feelings of efficacy: without sufficient training in a new educational model, pedagogy, or curriculum approach, teachers feel they don't know *why, what,* and *how* to implement best practices to increase outcomes of all students.

Recent research in professional development suggests that in order to have any impact on student achievement, our teachers must receive at least fourteen hours of study in the same professional development focus area.[25] Teachers who receive significantly more professional development—an average of 49 hours a year—can significantly increase the outcomes for all students.[26]

Most districts do not allow even forty-nine hours in a year for all the initiatives, let alone one of them. If we continue to provide teachers with only a few hours of professional development a year in Universal Design for Learning (UDL), they will not have the necessary background or skills to implement it effectively. Because teachers are learners, districts must design professional development for them that allows them to activate their brain networks so they know *why* UDL is important, *what* the framework is, and most important, *how* to design curriculum and instruction with embedded options so all students can succeed.

So what are all these initiatives that are competing with UDL for professional development time and where do they come from? Reviewing every possible initiative would take a book in itself, and I'm guessing many of your affective networks would shut down if I went down that road. It is valuable to know, however, that generally, initiatives fall into some specific categories: standards, curriculum, and teaching strategies. Each of these categories will be discussed, but it's also important to know that all these categories stem from state and federal mandates, most notably the Individuals with Disabilities Education Act (IDEA), No Child Left Behind (NCLB), and the Every Student Succeeds Act (ESSA). They will only be discussed briefly.

In 1990, the Individuals with Disabilities Education Act (IDEA) was adopted to reinforce the right of every child, regardless of disability, to be educated with their peers who were not disabled in the least restrictive environment available to them. IDEA also gave parents a voice in the education of their kids. Because IDEA pushed for inclusion, or all students being educated together, many districts explored new curriculum programs, new schedules, and new teaching strategies that would allow teachers to educate all students together.

The next federal legislation that brought with it initiatives was No Child Left Behind Act (NCLB). Although IDEA brought students together, the outcomes for all these students were not the same. NCLB shed light on the unequal outcomes for different groups of students and sought to remedy the achievement gap by increasing transparency and accountability.

To increase transparency, states were required to report performance for student subgroups. The intent was to make schools, districts, and states more aware of the performance

of students at risk of failing and ensure that all groups make progress. If schools did not make progress for all students two years in a row, they faced sanctions, or punishments that could eventually result in being forced to replace the majority of staff and/or submit to state takeover. Enter the age of accountability and a focus on standardized testing, which still drives a lot of decisions in school districts.

No Child Left Behind got its name from its premise: that all students are capable of achievement proficiency on standardized measures by 2014. The deadline has come and gone, and the achievement gap is still very much present. In short, NCLB failed to yield the results it set out to accomplish. As a result, the Every Student Succeeds Act (ESSA), adopted in December 2015, replaced NCLB. Although ESSA endorsed universally designed curriculum, instruction, and assessments, we haven't seen any radical changes in standardized assessments, and so many districts are still focusing improvement efforts on increased test scores without a specific emphasis on UDL.

UDL VS. STANDARDS AND CURRICULUM

Todd Rose, author of *The Myth of Average* and director of the Mind, Brain, & Education program at Harvard University, notes: "Many people tend to confuse standards and standardization. It's good to have common standards even in a more personalized learning environment, but how we measure them has to responsive to individuality."[27] Even though standards may have a bad reputation, it's important to note that standards don't create a rigid education for our kids. Standards are merely the destination on a journey. If learning is a road trip, the standards are merely the endpoint, but they do not determine the route a student takes.

WHY DO WE HAVE STANDARDS, ANYHOW?

Growing up, my family loved road trips. I fondly remember climbing into the Suburban, pillows and blankets piled to the ceiling, to drive from Seekonk, Massachusetts to Orlando, Florida; Duck, North Carolina; or Eugene, Oregon. Although the destination was important, that wasn't the best part. For us, it was always the journey to get there. Mom would stop by AAA and pick up Triptiks, that is, maps with possible routes highlighted in pink. As we were traveling, we'd often stop to monitor our progress and make a new plan.

"We're only two hours from Mt. Rushmore. Let's just take a detour!" Other times, it was completely random. "If the next song on the radio is sung by a man, we eat at the first restaurant we see. If it's a girl, Mom gets veto rights." Starting off in a small town in Massachusetts left us with thousands of possibilities to arrive at our destination.

The same is true with teacher expectations and the standards that drive the design and delivery of instruction. Think of standards as the destination on a GPS. Teachers are required to design curriculum and instruction so that students can achieve those standards, but like my childhood road trips, there are many possible routes with detours and stops along the way. Unfortunately, many teachers don't appreciate that there are so many possible journeys because the curriculum they are required to use provides a map with only one route.

All curriculum standards, including Common Core, outline specific knowledge and skills students should acquire in each grade. Some opponents of the Common Core argue that the Core is a curriculum that exposes students to inappropriate content or teaching methods. This is not true. An examination of any college and career standards, including the Common Core, will reveal a collection of standards, or skills, that students need to become knowledgeable adults. Instructional strategies and curriculum are not outlined in these standards. You will not see a required reading list or an outline of suggested teaching methods. This being said, schools often adopt curriculum, which may create a "one-size-fits-all" approach to meeting those standards.

For example, the Common Core Mathematics standards outline two critical areas of instruction for second-grade students: "(1) extending understanding of base-ten notation; (2) building fluency with addition and subtraction." In Texas, a state that did not adopt the Common Core, the standards are similar: "The primary focal areas in Grade 2 are making comparisons within the base-10 place value system, solving problems with addition and subtraction within 1,000, and building foundations for multiplication."

What you will notice is that there are no math problems identified in these standards. That is true of all standards. So, where do these math problems come from? They come from the textbook publishers. Textbook publishers review the standards and create problems, which may or not actually align to the standards. A recent study from Ed Reports examined twenty-six kindergarten–eighth-grade math programs and determined that fourteen of the programs did not align to the Common Core math expectations in a single grade. Only two programs were in full alignment with the standards.[28]

Because textbook publishers design curriculum, math problems can be evidence of a faulty interpretation of the standards. This leads to the next question: why did a school district adopt a program that does not align to the standards they are working toward? There are countless reasons that all lead back to initiative overload.

Sometimes, schools, administrators, or teachers don't have enough time to evaluate their standards and what students need to know or be able to do, so they may move forward with the adoption of a curriculum that doesn't teach students exactly what they are supposed to know. Once teachers have this curriculum, they are then required to spend significant time to learn how to deliver this curriculum to students before they truly understand the standards.

Interestingly, this was one of the great controversies surrounding the rollout of Common Core. Critics argued that teachers weren't given enough time to prepare for the new standards and students were impacted as a result.

What is critical here is to know that there are many more pieces to the puzzle than it appears. So how does this situation relate to the difficulty of adopting UDL?

Imagine for a moment that a curriculum is in fact aligned to the state standards—because either teachers are encouraged to design their own curriculum (which takes a tremendous amount of time), or the district adopted curriculum from an education publisher that invested enough time to create an aligned product.

Regardless of what a teacher is using, he or she has to spend more time to determine how that curriculum is going to be universally designed. No curriculum program is endorsed as being universally designed. As a result, teachers first have to learn their standards, and then they have to learn about the curriculum, and then understand how to deliver it in a universally designed way. That assumes, of course, that they already know what UDL is.

To provide an analogy (because you know I just love them!), imagine that you own a bakery and your specialty is cakes. You have a client who has a very clear goal: that you create the most delicious macaron on the planet. Since you're more of a cake expert, you spend time learning everything you can about how to make a macaron so that you understand the end goal. Once this is clear, you take the time to learn how to make macarons and you're pretty proud of yourself. Now, you have to squeeze in your macaron making because you're already super busy with your cakes—but you find the time and you understand *why* you need to make the macarons (the client is a big spender!), *what* they are and all the possible flavors, and you know *how* to make them. Just as you start making them, the client comes in and says, "I'm so glad you have that down. Now, you have to use all the tools and techniques you have, but you have to make the macrons exactly like Pierre Hermé, who by the way was voted the world's greatest pastry chef in 2016 by the World's Best 50 Restaurants."

That's a little bit what it may feel like to be a teacher who finally is implementing a curriculum and then UDL hits the radar of the school district. Again, the curriculum certainly can become universally designed—any curriculum can with the infusion of enough options, but the process no doubt takes time—and time is what all teachers are always short of.

However, if schools can prioritize initiatives and provide teachers with the time they need to personalize their journey to implement UDL, they will have engaged teachers who are committed to the UDL journey. Without a focus on both teacher and student learning, you may have disengaged, overwhelmed teachers, who do the best they can with what they have.

UDL VS. THE "OTHER" FRAMEWORKS

Like UDL, other educational frameworks strive to help all students succeed. One in particular is a critical obstacle to UDL implementation: differentiated instruction (DI). Indeed, teachers who are familiar with DI often confuse it with UDL. The two frameworks are similar, and can complement each other, but they are not the same. I believe it is important for teachers and parents to understand the differences, and to advocate for a UDL approach.

With DI, teachers respond to students to provide them with differentiated support. For example, students are sometimes put into different groups and given different opportunities to learn based on perceived ability. If one or two students have been deemed "struggling readers," they might be grouped together, as if they are the same. Other students might be considered "advanced students." These labels are not necessarily helpful unless both teachers and students have an opportunity to self-reflect and make choices for themselves to personalize their learning.

When teachers personalize learning for students without encouraging them to self-reflect and help to choose the path, teachers may make choices that disengage students. The process of making these decisions is a little like picking out ice cream for your kids. If you don't ask them what they like, and you make your best educated guess based on years of experience with your children, you can still get it wrong. To proactively plan for variability, student voices are considered in the design and delivery of their education in UDL.

In a DI curriculum, a teacher creates lessons and assessments with various levels of challenge and distributes them to students, based on their perceived level of ability. With UDL, a teacher designs a lesson with options and varying levels of challenges and then encourages all students to make their own choices. As students begin their learning journey, a teacher becomes a coach and can differentiate responses to students as they provide feedback and push every student to be more creative and more successful than the day before. Without UDL as a foundation, students often lose the opportunity to access all the same options as

FOR EMILY   FOR GEORGE   FOR MASON

their peers, and that, in itself, affects their engagement and achievement.

As you learned with the cookout analogy, UDL fosters the art of creating one lesson plan with enough embedded scaffolding and choice that every student receives the same options and can challenge himself or herself. There are no labels in UDL. There are only fabulous, amazing students with different levels of variability. Both frameworks provide options, but only UDL provides the same choices to all learners.

Now that you see what teachers are up against, it's probably clear why so many of our nation's teachers are overwhelmed, overloaded with initiatives, and unable to commit the time necessary to implement a new framework. It's not that they don't want to transform teaching and learning, even though, that, in itself, is hard. In my experience, once

teachers learn about it, they often set a goal to begin implementation. Unfortunately, time is often a significant barrier and they have to spend so much time learning about other initiatives, new standards, and new curriculum that they simply don't have an opportunity to become expert learners themselves and begin to implement UDL in the ways that are most relevant, authentic, and meaningful for them.

But let me share this: when teachers are supported and schools and districts prioritize their initiatives and focus professional development on Universal Design for Learning (UDL), all students have better outcomes. Everything about a universally designed classroom is warm, welcoming, engaging, and rigorous and embraces the unique mix of challenges and strengths of all students. This is why, we as parents, who have a voice in the education of our children, must advocate for schools to focus on UDL implementation so that all of our kids have better outcomes and are prepared for their future.

Key Takeaways

- Teachers face many barriers that prevent them from implementing UDL, but as parents we can partner with schools and take action to help to eliminate those barriers.

- When teachers are provided with meaningful professional development in how to implement Universal Design for Learning, the outcomes for all students improve.

Chapter 6

UDL IN ACTION

A universally designed learning environment is one in which all learners are working toward similar goals, but they have different strategies and methods to arrive at the same destination. Firm goals and flexible means can take many different shapes. The only constant in a universally designed environment is that all learners feel valued, have choices, and experience learning as a process of trial and error, in which failure leads to self-reflection as yet another mode of learning.

UNIVERSALLY DESIGNED ENVIRONMENTS

Before we examine what a UDL classroom may look like, let's look at some examples of other universally designed environments—those that do a wonderful job of ensuring equal access and engagement for all.

One example of a universally designed system was my high school track team. First, in track, anyone could be a part of the team. There were no tryouts and no cuts, so it was clear that all were welcome. Also, although there were over 100 athletes and we competed in different events and had wide variability, we warmed up together every day. Coach Seal would start by sharing words of inspiration, athletes of the week were honored, and strategies for upcoming weeks were discussed. Then, we had an opportunity to choose our events for the week. He encouraged all of us to try every event, as he said that sometimes you'd be great at something you wouldn't expect. On his team, you couldn't just label yourself as a "hurdler" or a "thrower" and call it a day. I remember shot putters running the 4×100 relay and jogging through a mile course, because we were encouraged to try everything.

After we warmed up together, we had the ability to choose the group where we wanted to focus our workout. Those who wanted to throw the discus, the javelin, and the shot put headed to the weight room. Coach Seal would take those of us who wanted to hurdle to practice hip circles and perform endless box jumps. Distance runners would set out into the woods for cross-country adventures.

Sometimes, small-group instruction wasn't enough. At the end of practice, we were encouraged to reflect on our progress and seek out 1:1 help if necessary. While my friends hit the weight room, iced their legs, or cooled down, I worked on the high jump, trying to get my arch perfectly in the Fosbury Flop. The important thing was, I never missed any of the team-building time, or the small-group sessions if I needed them. Also, I got to make choices about the events I wanted to try and was always pushed to run faster, jump higher, and throw farther.

Now, imagine a very different type of practice. Imagine that from the beginning, the team was divided. The hurdlers were labeled and whisked away to a different area of the track, whereas the shot putters were sent in the weight room. There are huge limitations to this model. First, there would have been no community and no equity in the message we received, the warm-up we had, or the team strategy that was discussed. Our paths would have been decided for us, and we would've never had the options to try new events, meet new people, and become more versatile. When our students' paths are decided without their input, they are not yet in a universally designed system, but as with anything in life, a universally designed classroom is well within our reach.

YOGA AND UDL

You may also recognize another example of UDL in your neighborhood yoga class. Yoga is for anyone, regardless of fitness level or age. How is it that one class can accommodate people with such variability? When moving into asanas, or yoga positions, you always have a choice to do a pose at a specific level or with an adjustment. Take a look at one yoga pose—crow—demonstrated here.

This pose requires ultimate rigor, but in any class, modifications and accommodations are presented as choices without fail. Instructors explain that it's important to honor your body and make necessary adjustments so that you can experience the true purpose of yoga. There is never any one way to do a yoga pose. Additionally, any yoga teacher worth his or her salt understands that scaffolding is a crucial part of the learning process. (Scaffolding is a technical term for providing temporary supports that can gradually be taken away as students make progress.[29])

For example, the beginner has the option of modified crow, where the feet are still firmly planted on the ground. The pose does not require balance. As practice evolves and the body becomes stronger, beginners can shift more weight to their hands to move closer to the traditional posture. Those who need more of a challenge can channel their inner yogi and opt for a more difficult version of crow.

It doesn't matter where you start or end. All are encouraged to begin at the level they are at and move forward, and throughout the practice, yoga instructors provide mastery-oriented feedback to ensure that postures are aligned to maximize the benefits of the practice. This acceptance of variability and ongoing feedback make yoga a practice that challenges everyone simultaneously. Yoga has been practicing UDL for thousands of years. It's time that all classrooms provide students with the same sense of acceptance while working toward rigorous standards.

UNIVERSALLY DESIGNED CLASSROOM

When UDL is implemented in schools, there is a belief that all students are capable of learning and that instructional methods, when implemented intentionally, can help all students succeed. So what does a universally designed classroom look like? How does it function? How does it allow for variability and still enable all learners in any setting become expert learners?

First, in UDL-topia, where all the Guidelines are fully optimized, all students are educated together. Without a truly inclusive classroom, some students will never have the same options as their peers. Although a substantially separate classroom can offer choice, they are not the same choices as their peers. So, as a first step, a universally designed classroom values inclusion and all learners are present. Once there is a focus on equal access and equity, it's time to apply the UDL principles to the design and delivery of curriculum and instruction.

PROVIDE MULTIPLE MEANS OF ENGAGEMENT

In a UDL classroom, the classroom arrangement is set up for minimal distractions. There may be noise-canceling headphones, standing desks, comfy chairs or couches, soft lights, or a table of supplies and resources like rubrics and exemplars for students who need them so they do not need to interrupt the class. All students may have access to fidget tools; quiet music; sensory bins; and the ability to get extended time, take breaks, or enjoy snacks or chewing gum to help them regulate throughout the day. As you can imagine, a universally design classroom looks much different from the classrooms of the 1950s, where all students sat quietly in rows and waited for instructions from the teacher. Think Starbucks and the Google office. Those are the classrooms of the future.

In a universally designed class, the standard, or goal, is clearly defined every day. When the goal of the lesson is shared, students are encouraged to ask questions, talk to each, and share suggestions to make the goal relevant to them. When your kids come home from school, you may ask, "What did you do in school today?" In a universally designed classroom, they would not only be able to answer *what* they were doing, but *why* they were doing it.

A universally designed classroom is not a line in a factory—students are not all doing the same thing. As a result, teachers are rarely up in front of a classroom. Instead, they are often walking around to keep students on task and prevent frustration. Teachers provide words of affirmation, mastery-oriented feedback, exemplars, graphic organizers, and so forth to help all students make progress toward their own goals.

PROVIDE MULTIPLE MEANS OF REPRESENTATION

When teachers provide multiple means of representation, content and skills are presented in multiple ways with scaffolding available for all students. When students are learning, more than one presentation method is apparent: lecture, reading text, audio, and video (i.e., teacher reads directions while projecting them with an Apple TV, or students watch a video with closed captioning). Students will have a choice about the information and resources they want to explore or the format in which they explore it. Instead of reading silently out of a tattered paperback, for example, students could have the option to read aloud with a peer, read on an IPhone, listen to an audiobook, or listen to the teacher read. Alternatively, teachers may provide stations where students can learn information on their own (i.e., read a text, view a video, listen to audio, or work in a collaborative group). Students also have daily access to the use of diagrams, charts, and images as well as other reference materials to help support their comprehension. They do not have to rely solely on text or lectures to build understanding.

PROVIDE MULTIPLE MEANS OF EXPRESSION

When we, as parents, think of tests, we may cringe. We shouldn't have to. To begin, any assessment that informs instruction is super valuable, and these are often administered before teachers begin a unit of instruction. Sometimes these assessments are called diagnostic assessments and other times they are called formative assessments, but the purpose is the same. When these assessments are given, teachers use the data and results to inform instruction, as they become aware of students' strengths and areas of weakness; this knowledge allows them to create more meaningful, relevant choices as the lesson continues. Giving students a choice assignment before or during a unit increases engagement, removes barriers, and allows students to practice self-direction and creativity as they share what they know.

Once students have learned material through access to a universally designed curriculum, teachers can give summative assessments, which measure a student's growth since the formative assessment. Both formative and summative assessments can take many different shapes. As long as the product allows teachers to assess student learning in response to specific standards, to see that they can express and apply what they have learned, the assessment is doing its job.

One type of summative assessment that is particularly controversial is the standardized achievement test. The limitations of standardized achievement tests aside, for students who are at risk of failing, a challenging, universally designed curriculum is crucial for success on these tests. This is not to say that any teacher should "teach to the test." Instead, teachers should focus on standards and actively involve students in learning by providing them with choices to personalize their classroom experience.

Standardized tests are a reality, and although they may not be universally designed, we are getting closer every day to more universally designed tests. Regardless, standardized tests are designed to measure student knowledge and understanding of state standards. If teachers design and deliver a universally designed curriculum embedding UDL, students will become self-directed, motivated learners; creative and practical problem solvers; and critical thinkers who have an understanding of the knowledge and skills they have been taught. These students will perform well, even if the tests have barriers. As Jon Mundorf, a teacher at the University of Florida's P. K. Yonge Development Research School, says, "I would rather teach in an accessible way to an inaccessible test, than in an inaccessible way for an inaccessible test." Knowing this, you should embrace that UDL never suggests that teachers "teach to the test" to increase student outcomes. Rather, UDL is concerned with students involved in deeper learning that carries over to success on a variety of measures.

When teachers are responsive to standards and understand the purpose of them, they offer engaging choices to assess the understanding of their students: art exhibits with written rationales, poems, podcasts, simulations, mock interviews, poetry slams, blogs, skits, lab reports, presentations, debates, and so forth. All of these enable students to express their knowledge in ways that will reflect on their progress.

Let's examine a high school math lesson so you can again experience what a UDL lesson looks like in action when there are multiple means of engagement, representation, and action and expression. The course is tenth-grade Algebra II, and students are working on the concepts involved in exponential growth and decay.[30]

The teacher begins the class by letting his students know that he has received a very interesting email stating that he will make a lot of money quickly if he does the following:

1. Send $10 to the first person's name on the list (which has 10 names on it) in the email

2. Take that person's name off the list

3. Add her name to the bottom of the list

4. Send a new email with this information to five new people.

The teacher gives the students a few minutes to discuss in small groups what they think will happen if the new email is sent. He circulates to ask a few questions such as *Will I make a lot of money?* and *How many people do you think will my name will get sent to?* as a way to encourage a deeper discussion.

Students are then given the task of creating a mathematical model to share how much money their teacher will supposedly make if this "scheme" is followed as directed, but they are encouraged to work independently or together to determine how they will figure out the answer. The teacher is clear that there is no right or wrong way to calculate the answer—many mathematical models may be appropriate.

In this example, where students are investigating a "get quick rich" scheme, the teacher encourages students to solve the problem, but he also needs to provide students with options so they can make meaning of the problem. The teacher identifies resources that students may use as support such as a chapter in the textbook, an online lecture, and an exemplar from another class. Some students choose to work in groups whereas others choose to work independently to complete the task. Their teacher circulates to clarify mathematical questions and to provide advice, mini-presentations, and lectures to students as requested.

Students are encouraged to share their work by creating a spreadsheet, including mathematical formulas, a graph including equations, or a written description of the model.

As students share their completed work, some with visuals, written examples, or multimedia presentations, the teacher leads a discussion about the similarities and differences between their models, noting the mathematical representations found within each model. After this discussion, students can review and revise their work before submitting it for a test grade. In this scenario, the process of learning and the expression of that learning becomes their assessment.

In this example, students are applying rigorous math concepts to an authentic task. As students are working, they are encouraged to make meaning by using multiple representations and they have opportunities to collaborate and receive mastery-oriented feedback from the teacher. Ultimately, however, students must create a mathematical model to express their understanding, so the teacher provides options for that as well.

As you can visualize, the teacher is not at the front of the class showing students what to do and then handing out worksheets so they can practice. Instead, the teacher provides an authentic assessment, the tools and supports students may need, and his presence to help to answer questions, provide motivation, and clarify expectations. In short, the students are doing more work than the teacher, which is what authentic assessment, twenty-first-century thinking, and UDL are all about. Success isn't a passive endeavor; neither is a UDL class.

UNIVERSALLY DESIGNED HOMEWORK AND SUMMER READING

Teaching and learning isn't just confined to the walls of a classroom. Robert M. Pressman, director of research for the New Center for Pediatric Psychology, and his colleagues published a study in the *American Journal of Family Therapy* titled, "Homework and Family Stress: With Consideration of Parents' Self Confidence, Educational Level, and Cultural Background."[31] From the title, it's clear that homework affects us just as much as it affects our kids. As much as students may struggle with school, the ritual can cause significant stress in our lives. If you have a student who struggles or who is disengaged in learning, you may dread the nightly homework routine. As a result, you probably find yourself Googling ways to improve the whole experience. Although there are definite strategies for you to universally design a student's homework space, if the assignments aren't universally designed, it could still be quite a challenge to make the best out of the situation. The good news is that when teachers and schools implement UDL, their homework practices begin to align to the UDL Guidelines. As a result, student engagement and coping increase, and our family stress level decreases.

Before diving into how to universally design homework, it's important to first answer the question, "What is homework?" One of the most important issues to consider when examining homework expectations is the type of homework that is assigned.[32] So often, we as parents focus on the amount of time it takes to complete homework without considering its purpose. Homework is a type of assessment, so quality homework assignments have a significant purpose and offer students opportunities to reach goals and reflect on their learning process. All three types of homework can meet these criteria if they are proactively designed. There are three different types of homework: practice homework, preparation homework, and integrative homework.

PRACTICE HOMEWORK

Practice homework is when students learn content and skills in class and then are expected to return home and practice. You probably are familiar with the drill on these types of homework. Spelling lists, math worksheets, vocabulary activities, and instrument practice are examples of practice homework. Much recent research has focused on practice homework and its inability to result in meaningful gains for students. In short, students are expected to use rote practice repeatedly, which doesn't activate their affective network. This is not to say that there is no benefit to practice homework. Rather, it's important that practice homework is not just "busy work" or rote memorization because these skills aren't valuable for students in their future.

Major advances in technology have made memorization less and less important. With computers and libraries embedded into our iPhones, we can look up the information we need in a second. In the future, it's not what you remember; it's the skills you use as a lens to critically think about resources you explore. Greg Satell, a business writer who regularly contributes to the *Harvard Business Review* and *Forbes*, cites the problem with much of the practice work that is assigned to students: "The truth is, there is little taught in school that today can't be handled with a quick Google search and an Excel spreadsheet."[33] The reason for so much practice work is that many teachers aren't aware of alternatives to teach students the content. UDL provides them with a blueprint to begin to make all assessments, including homework, personalized and meaningful.

When practice homework is personalized, for example, students may have the option to practice math equations or vocabulary they need in order to meet a specific goal. This makes the practice more meaningful because students have to think critically about what they need, and then they know *why* they are doing it.

PREPARATION HOMEWORK

Preparation homework includes such tasks as targeted reading and studying because students are preparing for future lessons or building fluency that will allow them to access more rigorous content in the future. Before moving on, it's important to unpack the term "reading" and how it's evolved from traditional education. "Reading" no longer means simply decoding words. Rather, "reading" is about closely analyzing and interacting with resources. To "read" is to absorb and interact with ideas. Ideas can speak to you, prompt you to share ideas, inspire you, or infuriate you. Just as human beings need to learn social and people skills to develop relationships, students need to learn analytical skills to have a relationship with the resources they explore to build their knowledge. It's important to note that reading has consistently been shown to affect student achievement positively, especially when students have the opportunity to choose resources that are meaningful and relevant to them. This is especially true when parents support their kids with reading.

Interestingly, one of the most important ways to support our kids' success is to read to them, and surprisingly, it's not because great readers are more successful. It's because people who read more become more integrated thinkers. Long story short, even if reading is not assigned as preparation homework, reading should become a part of your nightly routine. Now, with technology, there are so many additional options if you don't have the time to read while juggling sports, homework, work, and dinner. Consider downloading the app Overdrive to download audio books for free from your local library. When you're driving to and from soccer practice or dance rehearsal, or dropping your son or daughter off with friends, you can have them "read" a book.[34]

If you're thinking that your son or daughter doesn't love cozying up with a good book, think of reading using the UDL lens. Standards now acknowledge "text" as a much broader definition including speeches, poetry, maps, artwork, timelines, data, videos, and political cartoons.[35] Reading is an opportunity for learners to explore the unknown, think differently, and build new ideas.

If you have teenagers, you're probably thinking that the idea of snuggling and reading, in any way, shape, or form, would be torture to both you and your child. The good news is that when students get older, the best thing you can do to help students succeed in reading is to discuss movies, books, and current affairs with your kids. Sit down together and watch the nightly news, visit local museums and analyze paintings and exhibits, or attend concerts together and discuss the power of the music. All of this falls under the umbrella of "reading" today and into the future. Teaching kids about the world gives them a huge step up in their education.

INTEGRATIVE HOMEWORK

The last type of homework, integrative homework, is when new knowledge is applied in long-term projects such as essays, science experiments, and student-directed activities. Integrative homework generally has options for students to apply what they have learned in creative projects. Sometimes this is referred to as "project-based learning." Project-based learning is when teachers design learning opportunities so that students are empowered to complete assessments for purposes beyond school.

One example of a project-based learning project is a park improvement project designed for elementary school students. The goal of the unit was to help students become active, responsible citizens. They began their journey by visiting local parks or public spaces to determine how the spaces could be improved. Students then collaborated to create presentations to give to local officials (and they had the opportunity to actually give the presentation!). Finally, each student wrote a letter to a government official to outline the community's need and their proposal. As you can see, project-based learning is one example of an integrative assessment that has a clear purpose, is authentic, and requires students to apply knowledge in meaningful ways.[36]

Another example of an integrative homework assignment is the high school summer reading project in Groton-Dunstable Regional School District. The project, dubbed "Summer Language Exploration," epitomizes the goal of universally designed homework. The high school English department, led by chair Kelly Cook, helped pen the introduction to the assignment: "We used to limit this assignment to summer reading only, but we know that many students are ardent viewers, creative writers, journalists, movie makers, actors, vocabulary vultures, conversationalists, storytellers, and more. We want them to tap into their passions, as long as they play with language. This approach follows the philosophy of Universal Design for Learning." Because they were empowered with professional development, given the time to learn about UDL and create an authentic product, treated like professionals, and supported by administrators and parents to make choices that would best meet the needs of their students, they created an assignment that surpasses the quality of any summer reading assignment I have ever seen.

The journey to this amazing experience started last summer when they participated in professional development in UDL. As with all educators who are given the time, resources, and support to learn about UDL, they took the three principles and Guidelines and made magic. Together as a department, they redefined summer literacy for their students, without ever being asked, but I argue their work is even bigger than that. Their Summer Language Exploration is a model of collaboration, of creativity, and of how engaging learning can be when students are provided with rigorous, authentic, personalized options and teachers are empowered to use their expertise to ignite student passion in learning. In short, it is an exemplar of what a universally designed homework assignment can be.

Throughout the Exploration assignment, students were encouraged to choose meaningful opportunities to interact with language. When looking at just the reading options, students had the following choices, although they could also choose to listen or attend a live event instead. Check out a sampling of the options and consider how much more authentic the options are than the traditional book list.

- Create your own book club. Get together with a group of friends to read a novel or nonfiction book released in 2016. Video record part of your book club discussion, create a trailer for the book with yourselves as characters, vlog a review, or blog a review.

- Read to a blind person (through the Mass. Association for the Blind and Visually Impaired at *https://www .volunteermatch.org/results/opp_detail.jsp?oppid=281126*), a child in a pediatric waiting room (through Reach Out & Read at *www.reachoutandread.org/join-us/volunteer/*), or someone else who would like to be read to on a regular basis. Keep a journal about your experience.

- Read the newspaper. Get a free online student subscription at the *Boston Globe* or *Boston Herald*. Blog about what you read, write a letter to the editor based on trending topics, or listen to "Wait . . . Wait! Don't Tell Me!" (*www.npr.org/programs/wait-wait-dont-tell-me/*) on National Public Radio (NPR), and write about how well you did on the weekly quizzes.

- Read with the Groton Public Library. Participate in "Groton READS, Get in the Game: READ!" at *http://gpl.org/events-and-activities/grotonreads/* (for grades 6–12), or if you're old enough, "Exercise Your Mind: READ!" at *http://gpl.org/events-and-activities/summer-reading/* (ages 18+). You can also join an adult book group (Mystery or Great Books at *http://gpl.org/events-and-activities/book-groups/*) or check out one of the YA Book Club Kits in a Bag with your friends. Write about your experiences sharing and talking about books in a community.

- Choose a book to read with your family and discuss. (Scholastic at *www.scholastic.com/100books/* and Good Reads at *www.goodreads.com/group/show/95242-best-book-club-family-friendly* have good suggestions.) How did the shared experience affect the quality and types of interactions you had in the family unit?

- Read a genre or a topic you wouldn't normally explore deeply (poetry, how-to, plays, screenplays, nonfiction, collected essays, adventure) and stick with it. Write about your challenges and victories.

- Go on a quest for cash by reading an Ayn Rand novel and writing about it. Depending on your grade, you can enter contests for $2,000 (*https://www.aynrand.org/students/essay-contests#anthem-1*), $10,000 (*https://www.aynrand.org/students/essay-contests#thefountainhead-1*), or $20,000 (*https://www.aynrand.org/students/essay-contests#atlasshrugged-1*), no strings attached, if you write a winning essay. Certainly, someone at Groton-Dunstable is up to the task!

This rock-star department created equally amazing options for students to write, speak, perform, listen, delve into language, attend a live event, view or play, or create with media arts. You can access the full assignment at *www.katienovaudl.com*.

Using the UDL lens, you can see that learning environments, lessons and units, assessments, and homework can be wildly engaging when teachers optimize student choice and value each student's variability. As we say in UDL, it's all about firm goals and flexible means. When educators start by focusing on the *why*, and are given the professional development to design multiple opportunities for *what* students will learn and *how* they will learn it, your students will be better for it.

As parents, we have firm goals for our kids, and those goals almost certainly include being successful in school. We know how important education is to future success, and we want that for our kids. Unfortunately, when students aren't given meaningful options, they don't have the opportunity to personalize their journey, and success isn't always an outcome. As a result, we watch our kids struggle; we listen to them complain about how they are overwhelmed, bored, or stressed; and we wonder why they can't be more engaged. The answer is because their education isn't universally designed—*yet*. We need to take steps so that our schools know about UDL. We also need to advocate for the changes and support the transition to more self-directed learning by building a growth mindset and a culture of risk and failure at home. There is too much at stake for our families if we don't.

Key Takeaways

- Universally designed environments provide options for all students to be successful and build critical skills for their future.

- Universally designed assessments have a clear purpose, foster student investment, and drive future teaching and learning.

- Visualizing what UDL looks like in practice will help you to support your child's teachers in implementing UDL in the classroom and supporting the transformation to student-directed learning at home.

Chapter 7

RAISE THOSE EXPECTATIONS

*A*lice Thibodeau died at the age of 95. Before she passed away, she faithfully read *Reader's Digest* aloud, played canasta, and reminisced about the last century and how "kids today" would be so much better off without all the "conveniences." She lost five siblings to the influenza outbreak, and you didn't see her grumbling about it.

Alice grew up in the Great Depression, worked in factories during the second World War, and one by one, watched all her friends die before her, but she would not give up. She pushed her red sparkling walker, dubbed "the Cadillac," through the assisted living facility wearing her high heels, and she loved to share stories about everything she had to overcome. There was a gleam in her eye as she reminisced about all she accomplished when no one thought she could. Once, in her early twenties, she worked in downtown Pawtucket, Rhode Island, which was a couple of miles from her house, so she took the bus to work. One morning, she missed the bus. She said, "If you want to be successful in life, you don't make excuses. You get your fanny to work." So what did she do? She kicked off her heels and ran all the way to work in her stockings on the asphalt roadway. She said proudly, "I wasn't even late." Alice Thibodeau was my grandmother; we called her Memere, and I am thankful for her legacy.

Memere had what we now call *growth mindset*. Growth mindset is a critical aspect of engagement, which is one of the three principles of UDL. If we want our kids to be successful, they have to learn how to sustain effort and persistence, even when things are hard, even when things aren't going their way, even when they miss the bus. As a parent, teaching growth mindset isn't comfortable. We ourselves need to adopt a growth mindset to help us cope while our little ones struggle.

Your reaction right now may be a prickling in your chest. We often don't want to see "our kids" and "struggle" in the same sentence, but if we want to raise self-directed, gritty adults who can cope when things get tough, we need them to learn to work through struggle. We also have to have high expectations and help to teach our kids that we believe they will accomplish their goals.

An article on Understood.org titled "High Expectations for All" says, "If we want every child to succeed, high expectations are critical. Research shows that if we expect children to fail, there's a good chance they'll fail. But if we expect them to succeed and if we give them the help they need, they'll shine in school and life." This is called a self-fulfilling prophecy.

It's important to remember that a self-fulfilling prophecy can be positive or negative. Positive effects are called Galatea effects, named after the statue in the Greek myth. In the myth, a sculptor, Pygmalion, creates a statue, Galatea, and falls in love with her. His desire for Galatea is so strong that he infuses life into her. All ends happily. Negative expectancy effects are referred to as Golem effects. In the Hasidic myth of the Golem, a mechanical creature is given life to serve its creator, but the monster becomes destructive and must be destroyed.

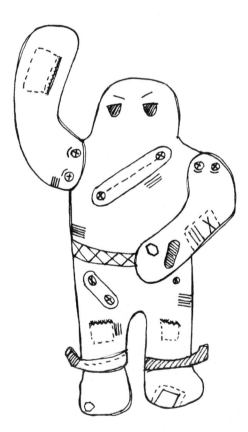

We need to have high expectations for our kids, share those expectations with them, and share them with their teachers, so that it will result in positive Galatea effects for them. One way we can do this is to help our kids build a growth mindset so they can rise to meet the challenges that life sets for them. This is a critical first step in setting high expectations for students.

We are all likely familiar with the classic child's tale *The Little Engine That Could*. Her mantra, which has become a cliché in the world of perseverance, "I think I can, I think I can," is a valuable message that we, as educators and parents, need to embrace.

Growth mindset is based on the simple premise that we are much more likely to succeed if we believe that effort, and not inherent skill, intelligence, and talent will result in success. The opposite of growth mindset, fixed mindset, is the belief that some things in life are simply out of reach. In classrooms, we hear students say, "I can't do that." When teaching graduate courses in UDL, teachers sometimes admit the same.

All teachers and students need to believe that they are capable of increasing their performance by applying necessary effort, seeking out information and resources, collaborating with more knowledgeable others, and repeating throughout the process, "I think I can."

If you think back on the greatest lessons you've learned in life, they were probably born from adversity. They were the times when things were down, and we should have quit, but for some reason, we were able to reflect, set a new goal, pick ourselves up, and persevere because we believed that we could do it. My parents were hugely instrumental in helping me to build this mindset. And you can have this same impact as well on your own kids.

In seventh grade, I tried out for the basketball team and was cut. I still remember that numbing feeling of staring at the list of names on the locker room door—scanning over and over again, willing my name to appear on that list. It did not. I remember going home that night and tucking myself in the corner of the kitchen, near the basement door, and crying.

At dinner, I remember lashing out at my parents, droning on that it was unfair that I didn't make the team. My parents had two choices about how to react. One would have taken me down the road of fixed mindset; the other, growth mindset. The fixed mindset route would have looked something like this: "I can't believe that [insert any name] made it and you didn't. I've seen her play. You're so much better than her. You are a great player. Clearly that coach plays favorites." This may have even taken the path of calling the coach to lambast his decision making and beg to let me make the roster. My parents did not take that route. Instead, they chose the path of growth mindset.

I still remember my mom leaning across the table and saying, "If you want to make the team next year, you have to practice more." As you can imagine, this ended in me storming up the stairs—"Even my own parents think I suck at basketball!"—but the fact that I still remember this twenty-five years later says something important about the message I received that day. I learned that making the team wasn't a lucky draw. It wasn't something I deserved. It was something I had to earn. And that pissed me off. Why? Because it would have felt a heck of a lot better to just make the team, play with my friends, and fantasize about my future in the WNBA.

You know what? I'm glad I didn't make the team. That taught me more than if I had made it. I was cut, and that hurt, but it made me want it more. I started practicing every day. I didn't quit. I saw what I wanted and I knew that if I wanted it, I had to keep trying. I wasn't there yet.

In eighth grade, I tried out for the basketball team again. I made the team. Over dinner, I bragged about how well I played during tryouts, and my dad, ever the growth mindset coach, said, "You have to keep practicing like you didn't make the team." Though I wasn't a fan of that mentality while I was growing up, later I could see that they planted something in me that allowed me to excel in life. They taught me at a very young age that if I wanted something, I had to work for it. I couldn't make excuses. I couldn't blame anyone. If I wanted something, I had to take the road less traveled, and as Robert Frost so eloquently penned in "A Road Not Taken":

> I shall be telling this with a sigh
> Somewhere ages and ages hence:
> Two roads diverged in a wood, and I—
> I took the one less traveled by,
> And that has made all the difference.

As a parent, take the road less traveled. Have high expectations for your kids and continue to motivate them as they make mistakes, fail, and try again. Give them options, encourage them to choose, and be there to motivate them when they struggle, but do not try to make things easier. When they are frustrated, continue to keep your expectations high, and they will rise to them. If we lower our expectations, or we allow our kids to avoid failure, we have failed them.

Jessica Lahey, author of the bestselling book *The Gift of Failure*, writes that embracing failure and mistakes are critical to learning, but as teachers and parents, we send an opposite message. In setting high expectations, we may share the message that success or achievement is the prize, not the journey to get there. Then, when things become challenging, we protect our kids by teaching them it's better to quit rather than face failure. This teaches kids to fear failure, which destroys their love of learning and prevents success, the very thing we're trying to build.[37]

In the book, *The Smartest Kids in the World: And How They Got That Way* Amanda Ripley discusses the power of parenting in raising students' academic achievement.[38] One observation she makes is that in countries where students surpass American students, the parents see themselves as coaches whose job it is to train their kids, and push them and "even bench them to prove a point" because they know that learning is difficult and kids have to learn to cope. In contrast, she notes that many American parents see themselves as cheerleaders who want everything to be easy for their kids.

Now that you know a little about how the brain learns, you know that learning requires hard work and success requires failure. Therefore, when we set high expectations, we have to acknowledge the many failures that students may face on their journey.

When classrooms universally design teaching and learning, all students can access a rigorous education, but it doesn't mean that learning is easy and they are always successful. The long-term destination is success, but there may be many micro-failures across the way. Even in a universally designed classroom, students will struggle, but it's a productive struggle that will lead them to reach their goals when expectations are high and the environment continues to provide motivation.

Therefore, the goal of a universally designed classroom is not to prevent students from struggling. Instead, it's to create goals that make students want to struggle because their journey will get them to a place where they want to be. When we advocate for UDL in our schools, we allow our kids to set meaningful goals that they want to achieve. Take, for example, the goal of "write an argument." In many cases, teachers will ask students to read an assigned text, choose a position, and defend it, using evidence from the text. If the content of the text isn't meaningful for a student, or if they struggle with writing, or if they haven't learned important rhetorical strategies that make arguments really effective, they complain that the assignment is too hard or too boring.

With a UDL makeover, however, a teacher could use the same goal but provide students with meaningful options. All students could be expected to "write an argument," but they could choose a topic that they are passionate about and an authentic form to share their position. Students could write a personal statement for a college essay and use rhetorical strategies to persuade an admissions office to accept them as a student. Still other students could join political campaigns and support a local candidate, write to an elected official, or blog about a topic they are passionate about. Students could "write" a script for a video infomercial or a podcast where they could share their position with the masses. The options are endless, and when students can personalize this experience, suddenly motivation increases. It's not because the task is easy—it's because they care about the goal. And that makes all the difference.

As parents, we need to work with schools so they give teachers permission to provide our kids with these options. We want our kids to learn how to be expert learners, and in addition to supporting skills, we can support this work at home too.

For decades, hundreds of research studies shared that more involved families have kids with higher grades, better behavior, and better attendance. This makes good common sense, but until recently, international studies didn't examine which types of parental involvement mattered most. In *The Smartest Kids in the World*, Ripley shares how we can get the most bang for our buck when we get involved in our kids' education. Spoiler alert: The most important support we can give to our kids is at home when we provide high expectations for them in all aspects of their lives and push them to succeed.

Parents and teachers have to believe that every student has amazing strengths and the ability to make choices about their own learning. Allowing kids to hone their skills, try and fail, and celebrate their strengths and their mistakes builds the motivation that is necessary for growth mindset and allows all students to reflect on areas where they can improve, and areas where they can contribute to help other students grow as expert learners.

If UDL is to be successful, we need to remember the 10,000-Hour Rule. Becoming an expert learner takes time and effort, but every one of our kids can get there. Without

UDL, students may not have the opportunity to practice critical skills in self-direction, creativity, and problem solving, and their engagement and achievement will suffer. As students struggle and become less engaged in their education, it creates a self-fulfilling prophecy because there is a belief that their lack of engagement and poor performance is because of their ability, or lack thereof. We need to break the cycle. It won't happen overnight, but it will happen. We have to believe that it's possible, and we can't rest until each one of our kids has the opportunity to see themselves in their education and know that the journey matters.

Key Takeaways

- A growth mindset is necessary for students to be successful in a universally designed learning environment.

- Regardless of variability, students and teachers need to have high expectations for all students and help them to build a growth mindset.

- When we have high expectations of our kids and we practice a growth mindset, our kids will more likely feel motivated to succeed.

Chapter 8

A CALL TO ACTION

A labyrinth is a complex, maze-like puzzle that can fluster even the most patient of trekkers. Case in point: In Greek mythology, Daedalus, a great inventor, designed a labyrinth for King Minos that nearly drove him to insanity. The King asked Daedalus to create a labyrinth to contain the Minotaur, the monster who was half-man, half-bull. The problem was that the King got stuck in the darn thing and barely got out. Poor Daedalus was just following orders. But when the King finally escaped from the labyrinth, he did what any self-respecting king would do—he jailed Daedalus, and his son for good measure.

Even though King Minos may have overreacted, we can all probably sympathize with this wary ruler. Sometimes in life, we see our kids struggling with school and we are driven to near insanity. We find ourselves going to great lengths to figure out how best to help them—but sometimes we make things worse. The good news is that with any puzzle, there is always a solution.

American education needs a transformation. Our current model of education does not meet the needs of all students. Less than half of our students are reading at grade level, our dropout rates are staggeringly high, and few students are truly engaged in their education. Additionally, even successful students often lack skills they will need in their future. If we want all students to find meaning in school, learn how to become expert learners, and be prepared for whatever future they dream for themselves, we need to move away from the outdated models that create barriers for the type of education our kids need.

For all these reasons, and more, we have to fix education. But we can't fix it alone. To get ourselves out of this labyrinth, which is preventing many students from being engaged and successful, we have to partner with schools and advocate for the changes *all* of our kids deserve.

Researchers have said for decades that schools need to partner with families to incentivize parents to advocate for their kids, but simply showing up at school activities will not improve their outcomes. We have to do more than show up. We have to get involved to help our schools, teachers, and students eliminate the barriers that are preventing them from implementing a universally designed education to our children.

You may be thinking: *she's crazy—I am so involved in my kids' lives! I barely have time to myself!* I get it. It's not that we're not involved in our kids' lives. It's just that we may not be involved in the ways that prompt positive changes in school, or that impact how our kids perform academically. In order to improve the achievement of our kids, we, as parents, need to become true partners with teachers and

schools. As the old adage goes, it takes a village to raise a child. We need each other.

To get involved in a more effective way that creates real change for all of our kids, we need to have high expectations for the nation's schools and our child's teachers—a collective growth mindset. If we don't, many students will continue to struggle academically, hate school, drop out, or be disengaged. We need to instill hope and motivation in our kids and in our teachers because success is well within their reach. Student success is achievable when every single learner has the opportunity to make learning meaningful. And this is not just wishful thinking. This is, as you learned in earlier chapters, the science of learning.

Activating all the networks in the brain is critical in helping our kids become the most successful, motivated, happy people they can be. To do this, our nation cannot continue to provide them with an education that tells them *what* they should know, *why* they should know it, and *how* they should express it.

What can you as a parent do to foster this change? On this journey, think of yourself as a trailblazer who, in the spirit of UDL, considers all of her (or his) options. You can engage in meaningful conversations with other parents and with educators. You can take actions to prompt school improvement, like making a briefing book or PowerPoint for administrators about UDL or sponsoring a speaker to introduce the ideas at a public forum. You can use some of the suggestions in the next section to engage your community.

To paraphrase John F. Kennedy for a moment, ask not what our schools can do for us but rather what we can do for our schools—because our kids deserve it. Consider the following buffet of options and put together a "plate" so you can take action in a way that is relevant, authentic, and meaningful to you. And please, share your journey.

DARE TO DIALOGUE

I recently read an article titled "Dare to Dialogue: Engaging Parents in System Change." Written for education administrators like me who want to create more meaningful partnerships with parents, the article discusses parent advocacy groups and what sets the most successful ones apart.[39] As I was reading, I couldn't help but think that the article should be read by parents, too, as it speaks to their (our) power:

> As professionals, we are satisfied when we know our clients and students derive benefit from our expertise, our concern, and often our love. Nevertheless, these benefits cannot begin to equal the power of determined parents whose love for their child causes them to be powerful advocates at all levels of our society. Parents can move mountains for their child...and they often do. They are frequently instruments of change in programs—for the better.[40]

As a mom, it gives me goosebumps. But time is of the essence and we as parents can't wait for schools to read that article and involve us. We have to insert ourselves into the dialogue in a meaningful way. As the author so eloquently penned in his title, we have to "dare to dialogue."

As a parent, you know your purpose. Any action you take is because of your kids, my kids, our kids. We live in a country where not all students have equal access to a rigorous, engaging, universally designed education, and we simply cannot allow that to continue. We all have the same purpose, the same goal. As discussed in the beginning of this book, we all want our kids to grow up to be successful, happy adults who can pursue and accomplish their dreams, find meaning, and overcome barriers, obstacles, and struggles. There is already so much we are doing to accomplish that goal, and after reading this, you've learned that there is something else you can do to take action. It's time to choose your next step.

- Consider starting a book club to inform more parents about UDL, or if you're not quite ready for one, choose a title for yourself. A number of publications are available that provide specific examples of the research behind UDL theory, UDL in the classroom, and the UDL design process (see "For Further Information" at the end of this book). You can even supplement with videos and/or journal articles. Regardless of the resources you explore, consider pairing your final meeting with a universally designed cookout!

- How about sharing or purchasing one of the suggested titles mentioned at the end of this book for classroom teachers or building administrators as an end-of-year gift? After all, there are only so many #1 teacher mugs a person can cherish! Pair it with a handwritten note, an email, or a visual that lets them know you appreciate how much is on their plate and how much they are trying to do for your kids.

- When your kids come home from school, you may want to ask them, "Did you have any choices today about how you learned or what type of project you completed?" If they say yes, be sure to send the teacher a note and share that you know all about UDL and that you're thrilled that it's being implemented. Teachers need love and support, and elevating and celebrating the great work they are doing is important to foster collaboration and community.

- If your child doesn't have an opportunity to personalize his or her learning, use it as an opportunity to send one or more UDL resources with a quick message like, "This is a really cool resource, and I was wondering if you've heard about UDL." If teachers haven't, that's a great opportunity to talk to principals to put it on their professional development radar so they can begin to find the time to make UDL implementation a priority. Administrators are busy too and are struggling with time and initiative overload, so sharing the benefits of UDL, and its importance for all students, will help start the movement.

- Speaking of professional development, how much time do your teachers have to learn about best practices like UDL? Often, you can review your school calendar and see when teachers have professional development days. Ask what they are learning about and try to learn along with them. Maybe collaborate with the PTO so parents and teachers can learn topics alongside each other.

- Share UDL with anyone who will listen: local parent advocacy groups or at a PTO meeting. If you're interested on research on its effectiveness or a sample parent presentation, you can access materials at my website *katienovakudl.com*—remember, we are in this together!

- Attend a town or a school board meeting. A school board meeting is a great place to discuss important educational issues, and yet many parents have never attended a meeting. In a recent research study, researchers examined the results from the 2012 American National Election Study, which asked a sample of nearly 6,000 Americans about their political participation. Less than a quarter of respondents reported attending a school board meeting over the past four years.[41] Don't only attend—share UDL!

- Consider contacting the chair of your school board to discuss the implementation of UDL in the district. Share what you know about UDL and that it is written into federal legislation. If he or she isn't receptive, *yet*, be patient. Share more resources, find a consultant to work with them, and bring more friends until they listen.

- If you homeschool your kids, your professional development is just as important. Consider collaborating with other parents to prioritize your own professional learning. Share articles, stories, and lessons and commit to creating a professional learning group where you and your peers ensure you have forty-nine hours of professional development in UDL so you can design meaningful options for your kids. That way, they can surpass all your expectations and find more meaning in the learning process than ever before.

- Given the power of social media, it's no wonder that parents can come together to change education. In 2013, a group of parents impacted the mayoral race in New York by coming together on social media and creating what they called a "Twitter battalion"—an email group of students, parents, and teachers who were ready to activate. If the city of New York can do it, so can we. Log on to social media and begin to use the hashtag #UDLparents—recruit teachers, friends, and your kids to start the buzz. If the chat is trending, it will make some noise! If you're going social, don't forget to tag me!

- Twitter: *@KatieNovakUDL*

- Facebook: *https://www.facebook.com/katienovakudl/*

- Instagram: *katienovakudl*

These options outline possible first steps, but it doesn't end there. This is only the beginning. As parents, we are involved from the time we first hold our little ones until our last breath. We want all our kids to navigate their world in the most authentic way, and you want their schooling to be meaningful and relevant, and to motivate and lead them to success. You now know that there is an education framework that provides a foundation to teach schools and teachers how to meet the needs of all our children while also teaching them important skills for the future, such as self-direction, creativity, and problem solving.

Being educated and active ensures all our kids—regardless of variability, regardless of where we live, and regardless of what their experience has been in the past—will be successful. Remember, as the quote we read earlier in this chapter says, schools "cannot begin to equal the power of determined parents whose love for their child causes them to be powerful advocates at all levels of our society."[42] It's time to move mountains. Please join me.

Key Takeaways

- Research suggests there are concrete steps parents can take to improve the education of their kids. The time is now.

- Your voice and your actions matter. You have the power to impact teaching and learning for all students.

- Remember, this is only the beginning. Together, we can get this done.

ENDNOTES

1   There are many great resources about Bell, but an excellent one to share with your kids is *Alexander Graham Bell: Making Connections* by Naomi Pasachoff (Oxford University Press, 1996), part of the Oxford Portraits in Science series. The series targets grades 6–9 but is good reading for adults, too.

2   Todd Grindal and Laura Schifter wrote about "The Special Education Graduation Gap" for the *Huffington Post* in 2016. See *www.huffingtonpost.com/todd-grindal/post_10880_b_8976972.html*.

3   These statistics are found in Cassandra Erkens, Tom Schimmer, and Nicole Dimich Vagle's *Essential Assessment: Six Tenets for Bringing Hope, Efficacy, and Achievement to the Classroom*, published in 2017 by Solution Tree (Bloomington, IN).

4   John Dewey's *How We Think* was published in 1910 by D. C. Heath & Co. (Boston). You can read it for free via Project Gutenberg: *https://www.gutenberg.org/files/37423/37423-h/37423-h.htm*.

5   Janine Willis and Alexander Todorov's study "First Impres-
    sions: Making Up Your Mind After a 100-ms Exposure to
    a Face" appeared in 2006 in *Psychological Science*, volume
    28, issue 7, pages 592–598.

6   Malcolm Gladwell's *Outliers: The Story of Success* was
    published by Little, Brown in 2008. The 10,000-Hours
    Rule originates in 1993 paper written by K. Anders
    Ericsson and colleagues called "The Role of Deliberate
    Practice in the Acquisition of Expert Performance." That
    paper appeared in the *Psychological Review,* volume 100,
    issue 3, pages 363–406.

7   Read Gladwell's "Complexity and the Ten Thousand Hour
    Rule" in the *New Yorker*, August 21, 2013 at *www
    .newyorker.com/news/sporting-scene/complexity-and-
    the-ten-thousand-hour-rule*.

8   Linda Dacey, Karen Gartland, and Jane Bamford Lynch's
    Well Played books of math games and puzzles are pub-
    lished by Stenhouse Publishers (*www.stenhouse.com*).

9   *Richie Parker: Drive* was made by ESPN in 2013. Look for it
    on YouTube.

10 For the discussion of the social and academic outcomes
    of students with disabilities, I drew on a 1995 article that
    more than twenty years later still holds up remarkably
    well: "Questions and Answers about Inclusion: What
    Every Teacher Should Know" by Bonnie B. Greer and John
    G. Greer and published in *The Clearing House: A Journal
    of Educational Strategies, Issues, and Ideas*, volume 68,
    issue 6, pages 339–342.

11 The quote is from the website of the Center for Universal Design, which Ron Mace founded at North Carolina State University. See *https://www.ncsu.edu/ncsu/design/ cud/about_ud/about_ud.htm*.

12 For more on UDL and its origins, see *Universal Design for Learning: Theory & Practice* by Anne Meyer, David Rose, and David Gordon, published in 2014 by CAST. You can buy the book or ebook editions, but you can also view a free multimedia edition online at *http:// udltheorypractice.cast.org*.

13 Brian Burnes, Dan Viets, and Robert W. Butler wrote *Walt Disney's Missouri: The Roots of a Creative Genius*, published in 2002 by Kansas City Star Books (Kansas City, MO).

14 See Timothy S. Susanin's *Walt Before Mickey: Disney's Early Years, 1919–1928*, published by The University Press of Mississippi (Jackson, MS) in 2011.

15 Science journalist Chris Berdik's *Mind Over Mind: The Surprising Power of Expectations* about the placebo effect was published by Current/Penguin Books (New York) in 2012.

16 Shanker is quoted in Barbara J. King's commentary titled "Why It's 'Self-Reg,' Not Self-Control, That Matters Most For Kids" found at *www.npr.org/sections/13.7/2016/07/ 07/484910409/why-its-self-reg-not-self-control-that- matters-most-for-kids*.

17 See Daniel Kahneman's book, *Thinking, Fast and Slow*, published in 2011 by Farrar, Straus, Giroux (New York), page 41.

18 Margery Cuyler wrote *Kindness Is Cooler, Mrs. Ruler* (New York: Simon & Schuster, 2007).

19 See the 2016 article "Face Perception and Test Reliabilities in Congenital Prosopagnosia in Seven Tests," by Janina Esins of the Max Planck Institute for Biological Cybernetics in Germany and her colleagues, published in *I-Perception*, volume 7, issue 1, pages 1–37.

20 See David Roger Fine's 2012 article, "A Life with Prosopagnosia," which appeared in *Cognitive Neuropsychology*, volume 29, issue 5–6, pages 354–359.

21 The American Institute for Learning and Human Development offers a succinct overview of multiple intelligences theory at *www.institute4learning.com/ multiple_intelligences.php*.

22 Jessica Lahey's article, "Should Teachers Be Allowed to Touch Students?," appeared on January 23, 2015 in *The Atlantic*. See *https://www.theatlantic.com/education/ archive/2015/01/the-benefits-of-touch/384706/*.

23 See the 1995 article by John A. Ross "Strategies for Enhancing Teachers' Beliefs in Their Effectiveness: Research on a School Improvement Hypothesis" in *Teachers College Record*, volume 97, issue 2, pages 227–251.

24 See Nelly Tournaki and David M. Podell's 2005 article, "The Impact of Student Characteristics and Teacher Efficacy on Teachers' Predictions of Student Success" in *Teaching and Teacher Education*, volume 21, issue 3, pages 299–314.

25 See Sara Hill's *Leap of Faith: A Literature Review on the Effects of Professional Development on Program Quality and Youth Outcomes*, published in 2012 by the National Institute on Out-of-School Time at Wellesley College.

26 See Ruth Chung Wei, Linda Darling-Hammond, and Frank Adamson's *Professional Development in the United States: Trends and Challenges*, published in 2010 by the National Staff Development Council (Dallas, TX).

27 The quote comes from an interview with Todd Rose published by the NEA at *www.nea.org/home/67995. htm*. His book, *The End of Average*, was published by HarperCollins (New York) in 2016.

28 See *www.edreports.org/math/reports/compare.html*.

29 See *http://edglossary.org/scaffolding/*. This site, *The Glossary of Education Reform*, put together by the Great Schools Partnership, is a wonderful resource to help parents understand terms and jargon used in schools.

30 This example comes from Karen Gartland, co-author of the *Well Played* series cited earlier.

31 Robert M. Pressman and colleagues published "Homework and Family Stress: With Consideration of Parents' Self Confidence, Educational Level, and Cultural Background" in 2015 in the *American Journal of Family Therapy*, volume 43, issue 4, pages 297–313.

32 See Pamela Coutts's 2004 article "Meanings of Homework and Implications for Practice" in *Theory into Practice*, volume 43, issue 3, pages 182–188.

33 See Greg Satell's article, "We Need to Rethink How We Educate Kids to Tackle the Jobs of the Future," published April 8, 2017 in *Inc.* magazine, *https://www.inc.com/greg-satell/we-need-to-educate-kids-for-the-future-not-the-past-heres-how.html*.

34 See Amanda Ripley's book, *The Smartest Kids in the World: And How They Got That Way*, published in 2013 by Simon & Schuster (New York).

35 Let teachers know about the Literacy Design Collaborative's LDC Template Task Collection 2.0, a fabulous planning resource found at *www.ldc.org*.

36 This example is cited in "Project-Based Learning Not Just for STEM Anymore," an article by literacy specialists Nell Duke, Anna-Lise Halvorsen, and Stephanie Strachan and published in the education magazine *Phi Delta Kappan* (volume 98, issue 1, pages 14–19).

37 See Jessica Lahey's *Atlantic* piece cited above.

38 See Amanda Ripley's book cited above.

39 See Patrick Graham, Sara Kennedy, and Johanna Lynch's 2016 article, "Dare to Dialogue: Engaging Parents in System Change," published in the journal *Odyssey: New Directions in Deaf Education*, volume 17, pages 1768–1771.

40 The quote cited in Graham, Kennedy, and Lynch comes from Janet DesGeorges, Sara Kennedy, and Noëlle Opsahl's *Beyond the IEP: Families and Educators Working Together in School Programs*, a booklet published

by Colorado Hands & Voices. You can find it at *www
.cohandsandvoices.org*.

41 See Andrew P. Kelly's 2014 monograph "Turning Lightning into Electricity: Organizing Parents for Education
Reform," published by the American Enterprise Institute
for Public Policy. Find it online at *https://www.aei.org/
wp-content/uploads/2014/12/Kelly_Turning-Lightning-Into-
Electricity.pdf*.

42 The quote is from Janet DesGeorges, Sara Kennedy, and
Noëlle Opsahl, as mentioned above.

FOR FURTHER INFORMATION

$\mathcal{T}$o learn more about Universal Design for Learning, check out these resources:

- *Universal Design for Learning: Theory & Practice*, by Anne Meyer, David H. Rose, and David Gordon.

  - This 2014 book published by CAST Professional Publishing gives a comprehensive look at the origins of UDL in the learning sciences and in CAST's work to provide people with disabilities with equal opportunities in education.

  - Meyer and Rose founded CAST, an award-winning nonprofit education organization, in 1984, and they originated the UDL principles and Guidelines.

  - You can buy print and ebook editions from major online retailers. There is also a multimedia web edition that can be read for free (with registration) at *http://udltheorypractice.cast.org*.

- *UDL Now! A Teacher's Guide to Applying Universal Design for Learning in Today's Classrooms*, by Katie Novak.

  - The revised and expanded edition published by CAST in 2016 provides practical insights and savvy strategies for helping all learners meet high standards.

  - The book shows teachers how to use the UDL Guidelines to plan lessons, choose materials, assess learning, and improve instructional practice.

  - Key concepts such as scaffolding, vocabulary-building, and using student feedback to inform instruction are discussed, as are tips for recruiting students as partners in the teaching process, engaging their interest in how they learn.

- I have co-authored two other books about UDL—*Universally Designed Leadership: Applying UDL to Systems and Schools*, written with longtime colleague Kristan Rodriguez, and *UDL in the Cloud*, which shows how to design online courses using UDL. The latter was written with Tom Thibodeau, who is assistant provost at New England Institute of Technology, a creative educator and thinker, and, oh yeah, my dad.

- In 2015, science journalist Chris Berdik (who is cited elsewhere in this book) wrote a piece for the online magazine *Slate* about UDL and CAST's work, tying it to social-emotional learning. It's at *www.slate.com/articles/technology/future_tense/2015/03/universal_design_for_learning_brings_emotions_into_education_technology.html.*

- The Harvard Graduate School of Education also published a nice piece about UDL: *https://www.gse.harvard.edu/news/uk/08/12/importance-universal-design-learning*.

- The National UDL Center—*www.udlcenter.org*— is in the process of getting an update, but some of the older materials online are still helpful for gaining an intro to UDL. The Center's YouTube page is a good place to start: *https://www.youtube.com/user/UDLCenter*.

- Loui Lord Nelson, an early adopter of UDL, has written a really great book, *Design & Deliver: Planning and Teaching Using Universal Design for Learning,* as has another early adopter, Patti Kelly Ralabate. Patti's book is *Your UDL Lesson Planner.* And now Loui and Patti have joined forces to write *Culturally Responsive Design for English Learners: The UDL Approach*, which shows how specifically to address the needs of English language learners by braiding two frameworks: UDL and Culturally Responsive Teaching.

- *Universal Design for Learning in the Classroom: Practical Applications* is a 2012 collection (Guilford Press) edited by Tracey Hall, Anne Meyer, and David Rose of CAST. The book considers UDL in a variety of content settings, including math, art, reading, history, and so forth. A new edition is in the works but the old one is still a valuable, readable intro to UDL in practice.

INDEX